the Spanish kitchen

the
Spanish
kitchen

explore the ingredients, cooking techniques and
culinary traditions of Spain, with over 100 delicious
step-by-step recipes and over 400 photographs

pepita aris

southwater

This edition is published by Southwater

Southwater is an imprint of Anness Publishing Ltd
Hermes House, 88–89 Blackfriars Road, London SE1 8HA
tel. 020 7401 2077; fax 020 7633 9499
www.southwaterbooks.com; info@anness.com

UK agent: The Manning Partnership Ltd, 6 The Old Dairy,
Melcombe Road, Bath BA2 3LR
tel. 01225 478444; fax 01225 478440
sales@manning-partnership.co.uk

UK distributor: Grantham Book Services Ltd, Isaac Newton Way,
Alma Park Industrial Estate, Grantham, Lincs NG31 9SD
tel. 01476 541080; fax 01476 541061; orders@gbs.tbs-ltd.co.uk

North American agent/distributor: National Book Network,
4501 Forbes Boulevard, Suite 200, Lanham, MD 20706
tel. 301 459 3366; fax 301 429 5746; www.nbnbooks.com

Australian agent/distributor:
Pan Macmillan Australia,
Level 18, St Martins Tower,
31 Market St, Sydney, NSW 2000
tel. 1300 135 113; fax 1300 135 103
customer.service@macmillan.com.au

New Zealand agent/distributor: David Bateman Ltd,
30 Tarndale Grove, Off Bush Road,
Albany, Auckland
tel. (09) 415 7664
fax (09) 415 8892

A CIP catalogue record for this book is available from the British Library.

Publisher: Joanna Lorenz
Managing Editor: Linda Fraser
Project Editor: Susannah Blake
Assistant Editor: Lindsay Kaubi
Photographer: Nicki Dowey
Home Economist: Lucy McKelvie

Assistant Home Economist: Emma McKintosh
Stylist: Helen Trent
Designer: Nigel Partridge
Cover Design: Balley Design Associates
Copy-editor: Rosie Hankin
Production Controller: Claire Rae

Previously published as part of a larger volume, *Spanish Food and Cooking*

1 3 5 7 9 10 8 6 4 2

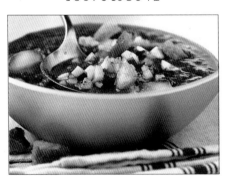

NOTES

Bracketed terms are intended for American readers.

For all recipes, quantities are given in both metric and imperial measures and, where
appropriate, measures are also given in standard cups and spoons. Follow one set, but
not a mixture, because they are not interchangeable.

Standard spoon and cup measures are level.
1 tsp = 5ml, 1 tbsp = 15ml, 1 cup = 250ml/8fl oz

Australian standard tablespoons are 20ml. Australian readers should use 3 tsp in place
of 1 tbsp for measuring small quantities of gelatine, flour, salt, etc.

Medium (US large) eggs are used unless otherwise stated.

CONTENTS

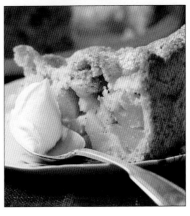

INTRODUCTION

The history and religion of Spain are visible on the plate. It is always true, to some extent, that what we eat says who we are. But in no country is it more obvious than in Spain. Ingredients, cooking methods and many recipes all have an easy-to-trace and fascinating past. And Spain's most famous foods – *chorizo, cocido, gazpacho, bacalao, paella* – have an encoded history.

MOORISH INFLUENCES

"A land which hovers between Europe and Africa, between the hat and the turban" was Richard Ford's description of Spain in 1845. The Moors invaded Spain from North Africa in AD711, and stayed for nearly 800 years. The Moorish influence is still evident today. To start with, a huge number of food words are derived from the Arabic: *aceite* (oil), *arroz* (rice), *albóndigas* (meatballs), *almendras* (almonds), *almirez* (the mortar) and *almuerzo* itself, the word for lunch.

In the mosques and palaces of Córdoba, irrigation systems were planned, making possible wonderful gardens such as the Generalife in Granada, as well as Valencia's rice fields. The valleys of the Guadalquiver

Above (left and right): Many dishes such as sardines en escabeche and rich fruit syrups show the Moorish origins of much Spanish food.

and Granada bloomed. The grey-green olive and the newly introduced almond transformed the landscape, while orange and lemon trees filled courtyards and surrounded buildings. New crops were planted, including sugar, spinach, aubergines (eggplants) and mint.

From the Moorish cuisine came new culinary methods – cooking in sealed clay pots and wood-burning ovens were introduced. The meat skewer and kebabs arrived, and *churrasco* (pieces of meat cooked on the barbecue) is still

a Spanish favourite. Frying with olive oil and preserving in vinegar (*escabeche*) were both Arab practices, the latter eagerly adopted by the locals for preserving surplus fish for a little longer. The mortar and pestle could grind nuts to a smooth cream, used to thicken chilled soups such as the almond *ajo blanco* (white garlic soup) or *salmorejo* (a cream of garlic, bread and vinegar). Both were forerunners of the classic chilled soup, gazpacho.

Many things that are now considered typically Spanish come from this era: almond pastries, fritters in honey, milk puddings, quince paste, peaches in syrup, iced sorbets, raisins and pine nuts used together in sauces, and the "caviar", botargo.

The spices brought by the Moors included cinnamon, cumin and nutmeg, served with chicken the way they are now, and the magnificent golden saffron. They enjoyed sour-and-sweet (*agridulce*) mixtures and anise bread. Look around in Spain now and you will find all these things still on the menu.

Left: The Spanish love to cook and eat outdoors, and cooking pieces of meat on skewers over a barbecue comes from the Moorish tradition.

Right: The slow-cooked stew of meats and chickpeas, cocido, *was inspired by the Jewish sabbath stew,* adafina.

CATHOLICISM CONQUERS

The *Reyes Católics* – the Catholic monarchs, Isabella and Ferdinand – conquered Granada, the last Moorish stronghold, in 1492. They threw out the Moors and the Jews, who were the Moorish managerial class, to make one united Catholic kingdom. The Jews, who had been in Spain for many centuries, left several imprints on Spanish cuisine, including *cocido* (meat and chickpea stew). The Christmas *roscón* has common features with the sticky braided *challah*, the Jewish Sabbath loaf.

The new foods enjoyed in this era were spectacularly different, favoured almost entirely for their religious orthodoxy. *Bacalao* (salt cod) was for Church fast days, of which there were some 200, when abstinence from meat – and sex – was required. Pork, which neither of the displaced peoples would have touched, became an integral part of Spanish religion, and therefore everyday life. Eating sausages became a statement of loyalty and proof of conversion to the Catholic Church.

Below: Of all the spices that the Moors brought with them to Spain, rich golden saffron is the one most distinctively associated with Spanish cooking.

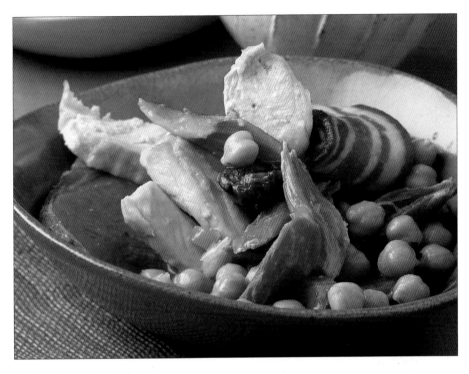

Cocido, the national dish

It is ironic that the *cocido*, that pot of long-cooked meats with chickpeas, is the legacy of a people whom the Spanish rejected. Its origins lie in the Jewish *adafina*, the Sabbath casserole, cooked the night before, and also served in three courses. *Pelotas* are

Below: Since the days of the Catholic kings, pork sausages such as spicy red chorizo have become the main meat eaten in Spain.

still added to *cocido* on big occasions. These are balls of minced (ground) meat or chicken livers, bread and pine nuts that echo the hamine eggs that the Jews added to *adafina*.

Adopted by the Catholic Spaniards, pork and sausages were added to the other meats in the *cocido*, as proof that the eaters were neither Jewish nor Muslim. Made almost entirely with meat, it was at first a thoroughly aristocratic dish. Then, as more chickpeas and potatoes were added, so it slipped down the social scale. Every region adds its own vegetables, and the further from Madrid, the more of a rural *puchero* (bean and sausage or meat stew) it becomes.

The Sephardim

This was the name given to the Spanish Jews; it is the Hebrew word for Spanish. When the Jews fled from Spain, they took with them many of its vegetables and dishes, including lentils, citron, fried fish, the boiling chicken with the bird's unshed eggs still inside, chicken with olives, and chicken soup with almonds.

HOLY SWEETMEATS

At one time, the Church employed one-tenth of the population in Spain, many of them women. In Old Castile and in the south, nuns turned to cookie- and sweetmeat-making for charity. Egg whites were used in sherry-making and the left-over yolks given to the convents. The nuns combined these with cheap sugar from Latin America to make little *natillas* (custards) and sweetmeats.

Today, you can still go to closed convents and place your order through the grille or put money on the shelf in a *tornador* (revolving door) and receive back goodies. The best-known of these are *yemas de San Leandro* (egg yolk balls). Christmas brings red quince jellies, coconut truffles, *mantecados*, *polvorones* and potato cakes called *cubilitos* (little cubes). Other delicacies include the almond and cinnamon cream known as *bien me sabe* (I know it does me good).

Below: Dried salt cod has been enjoyed in Spain for centuries. In times past, the dried fish was carried across the country by muleteers.

FOOD ON THE ROAD

Spain is a country of mountains, and of fierce regionalism. Nevertheless, it has always had its travellers. The muleteers of León were the equivalent of modern-day lorry drivers, criss-crossing Spain with their load of salt cod and news. They had their own recipe, *bacalao ajo arriero* (dry, hard fish rehydrated in a pot with oil and garlic), which is now often transformed into a Christmas *brandade* or into a tomato-based dish.

Tourism is not a new phenomenon in Spain either. Santiago de Compostela has been a major shrine for pilgrims for a millenium. In the 1550s, at the height of its popularity, up to two million people a year, from all over Europe, walked there south of the mountains on the *camino frances*, or along the coast. Scallop shells were their badge, but in their bags they carried bread and smoked sausage. At the pilgrim monasteries, crowds of up to 1,500 were fed on chickpeas and chard.

Another transient people, the gypsies (who originated in Egypt and India), arrived in the 1450s. They settled in Andalusia where they took up the jobs left vacant by the Moors and Jews. They also came to be featured in the folklore of the south by becoming the smugglers and bandits of the 19th century. They brought an element of improvisation to Spanish cuisine, which contrasted with the tradition of long-cooked stews.

Above (left and right): The tradition of sweet cookies and custard desserts was once the province of Spanish nuns, who made and sold them for charity.

FOODS FROM NEW LANDS

The introduction of new foods from Latin America after 1492 changed the Mediterranean diet for ever. Spain was transformed from being a bean, grain and meat-eating country, into a place where vegetables were widely enjoyed. An increase in population followed in Spain and Europe.

Chocolate and chilli peppers quickly became firm favourites in the Spanish kitchen: chocolate as a drink, and chillies as a condiment. Tomatoes were adopted and used in sauces, and the newly discovered varieties of beans became a firm fixture at the heart of Spanish cuisine. Potatoes, however, never displaced the great popularity of chickpeas, and corn was adopted only in Spain's fringes. (Could the reason for this be that tobacco was discovered on the same day – and the Spanish preferred the latter?)

From the east, the Portuguese who returned from China in the early 1500s brought with them sweet oranges. To this day, oranges are still known as *chinas*. The resulting orange trees, which now grow in such abundance all over Spain, have dramatically altered the landscape of the east and south coast.

Right and far right: Spain boasts the longest coastline in Europe and from two oceans come a vast array of fresh seafood, including scampi and sardines.

BETWEEN TWO OCEANS

Spain's longest frontiers are water so it is no wonder the Spanish are seafarers. Spain has always looked outward to the Atlantic as well as inward to the Mediterranean. First came shipping salt, whaling and fishing. Later Cádiz and Sevilla provided the ships and stores for "the Empire on which the sun never sets" – a phrase used to describe Spain before it was borrowed by the British Empire. In Spain, *América* refers to Latin America, which was open territory for the *conquistadores* (adventurers) to make their fortune.

Mediterranean links

Since the Phoenicians first arrived from the eastern Mediterranean and planted olive trees, Spain has long had links with its eastern neighbours. In fact, in terms of food influences, Spain has probably given more than it has received.

The Romans imported Spanish olive oil and adopted Spanish chickpeas to feed their armies. Under the Borgias,

Spain introduced beans to Tuscany – and possibly *sofrito* (fried onion-based dishes). When the kings of Aragón ruled Italy, saffron and short grained rice were planted, which were to become the base of the classic Italian dish, risotto.

France adopted mayonnaise, *aioli*, iced soups, chocolate, haricots and tomatoes, plus the beans and spices that transformed their *cassoulet*. With

France's culinary reputation, you might expect to find French dishes in Spain, but there are actually more Spanish dishes to be found in France. In return, from France, Spain received wine-making skills, including the technique of maturing wine in oak barrels.

Thanks to the Moorish culinary influence, a huge range of kitchen skills travelled via Spain to other countries.

Below: Chillies came from America and became a widely used condiment in Spanish food and cooking.

Below: Lemons were brought to Spain by the Moors, while sweet oranges were brought from China by the Portuguese.

Below: Spanish olives owe their legacy to the Phoenicians who first planted the trees there thousands of years ago.

THE REGIONS OF SPAIN

The Spanish regions are divided by many mountain ranges. This separates them geographically, but has also led to cultural differences as well. The climate, too, varies enormously, both across the regions and from winter to summer. Both these factors have contributed to the creation of distinctive local food traditions.

THE SOUTH

Typical images of Spain are of the south: blinding sunshine and a cool arch leading into a Moorish patio where a guitarist is quietly practising; white walls, covered with pots of bright geraniums; horses parading and girls in polka-dot flounced skirts. The great black bull silhouette that advertises Veterano brandy stands proudly on the rims of the brown *sierra* mountains.

Andalusia

This region encompasses the whole of the south coast, looking east to the Mediterranean from Almería province, south to Africa from Málaga and out to the Atlantic beyond Gibraltar. It embraces two sunlit worlds – that of the tourist beaches and another of fishing, farming and flamenco.

Water-splashing from fountains, running in rills through gardens, or poured from cans at night on to the green plants in every doorway – is the key to the region. For it was these fertile valleys that brought the Moors across the narrow straits from Africa. Now wonderful crops of asparagus and strawberries grow in the Guadalquiver delta and the *vega* of Granada. Valleys of tropical fruit face the sea, ripening in the glorious sunshine. Almería, with the help of irrigation, grows for export tomatoes and peppers. The grey-green olive grows where nothing else will, and orange and lemon trees, loaded with fruit, surround the villages.

The province is mountainous with many *sierras*: the Sierra Morena north of Seville and the Sierra Nevada south-east of Granada, where the Mulhacén rises 3,482m/11,420ft, its icy diamond piercing the sky beyond Granada. The *pueblos blancos*, white villages, cascade down the brown hillsides. This is the land where tapas were created – a little drink, a little food – as an unwinder at the end of a scorching day.

Andalusia's greatest foods are green olives and the scarlet, dried hams of the *sierras* – hence the name *jamón serrano*. A wide variety of shellfish are found in abundance in the warm Mediterranean, and from the Atlantic come big fish such as shark and tuna.

In this corner of the province are the sherry *bodegas*, cathedrals where oak barrels, stacked in dark tiers, mature the precious liquid. Sherry flies through the air when the *venecia* (a sampling can fixed on a long rod) dips into the butt and is poured in a graceful arc into a row of glasses held between the fingers of a master.

Splendid church processions and pilgrimages with ox carts, bull fighting and fiestas celebrating horses or sherry, all punctuate the year. They lend formality as well as colour to a region deeply committed to its folklore. Gypsies, especially in Seville and Granada, have created the rhythms of flamenco. They also have a reputation for improvising quick and delicious dishes.

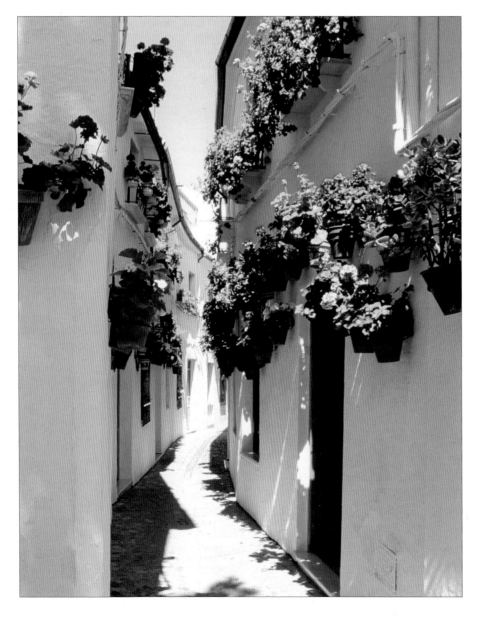

Left: Sun and shade, blinding white walls and pots filled with geraniums are typical of Andalusia's many villages.

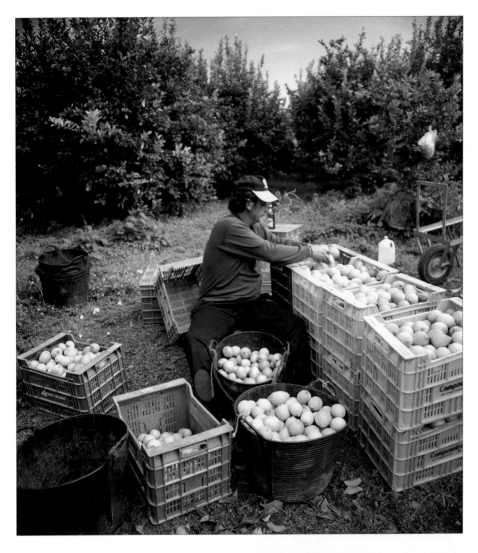

Above: Murcia's hot climate and lush plains produce nearly half of Spain's lemons each year.

Andalusia is said to be the "zone of frying"; certainly it is done superbly. But in the villages, old-fashioned stews of beans or chickpeas are just as common. *Gazpacho*, once the only daytime meal of poor labourers (who ate it again hot at night), is these days a chilled tomato and cucumber soup, wonderfully refreshing in the midday heat. There are many different versions of *gazpacho*, but all contain garlic, vinegar and oil.

Sangría, the chilled mixture of wine and citrus juice is another universally popular summer cooler. It belongs to a world of the *siesta* – afternoons of pure peace, when jobs can be put off until *mañana* (tomorrow).

Murcia

East of Andalusia lies Murcia, another Moorish province; indeed, the Moors ruled here, unnoticed, until 1609. This is another market garden area, with the *Huerta de Murcia* growing seas of bright green parsley and broad (fava) beans so tender they are cooked in the pod. It is said you breakfast twice here, once on chocolate and once on (bell) peppers. Stuffed peppers, tomato salad with cumin and an *escabeche* of aubergines (eggplant) with vinegar are popular. But the region is famous for its lemons, pickled capers and for Calasparra rice, Spain's best and ideal for paella.

Moorish dishes include *pastel murciano*, a pigeon pie with elaborate pastry that mimics the *b'stilla* of Morocco, desserts such as *arrope* and *jarabes* (fruit syrups), and *pan de higo* (pressed fig cake). The region also has a connection with Cuba, with dishes such as *arroz cubana* (Cuban rice).

In the salt lagoons of the Mar Menor, grey mullet are reared to eat and for caviar. *Lubina* (sea bass) baked in salt is an internationally acclaimed dish.

Below: Water was the key to the Moors' success in Andalusia and the fountains of the Genaralife in Granada irrigate one of their greatest gardens.

CENTRAL SPAIN

At 700m/2,300ft, the *Meseta* is the high heart of Spain and comprises nearly half the country. This is *Castilla* (of the castles), a great plain with Madrid in the middle, which divides into two rather different halves.

Northern Castile and León

Tierra de pan y vino (land of bread and wine) is one description of the Duero valley. Bread has mystical significance in the great grain plains of Old Castile. The bread basket of Spain produces round *hogazas*, big close-grained loaves, and houses retain their circular ovens, even when they no longer work.

Legumes are daily fare, well-flavoured with garlic. Chickpeas and lentils grow here, and white *alubias* that are used to make bean stews with oxtail or pigs' ears and sausage. The northern fringe, El Bierzo, is very wild, but known for *empanada de batallón*, a pie that gathers all the good produce of the region together – chicken, rabbit, frogs, chorizos and (bell) peppers. The old kingdom of León is deeply influenced by the French pilgrim route passing through it, which shows in foodstuffs such as sausages. Best known are Burgos's *morcilla*, a black pudding (blood sausage) with rice, and Cantimpalo's *chorizo*, Madrid's choice for their traditional stew-pot, *cocido*.

In the north-east, sheep graze happily in the summer, but winter is icy here and woollen blankets sell well. Soría and Burgos are important centres in this region. Sheep's milk is used to make cheeses – soft, white Burgos and the celebrated *manchego*.

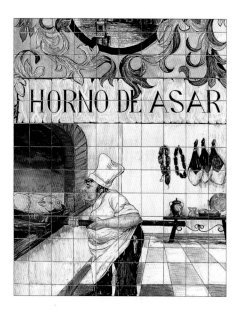

Above: Painted wall tiles in a Madrid restaurant advertise the wood-oven that is used to make celebrated roast meats.

The region is famous for its wood-fired ovens. In Sepúlveda they roast *lechazo*, milk-fed lamb, while further west in Arévalo and Segovia, *tostones*, tiny 15–20-day-old suckling pigs, are roasted to perfection. The best calves in the country are reared in Ávila.

Fritters, punch cakes and Tordesilla pastries appear in cake shops, while the many convents specialize in *repostería* (confectionery), including *rosquillas fritas* (fried rings), *pastas de té* (tea cakes) and *cocos* (coconut balls).

Madrid

Everyone in Madrid belongs to the country, so they say, and patronizes a regional restaurant. The city's dish is *cocido*, but *callos* (tripe) is so popular that it has moved from the home to become bar fare. Madrid's many restaurants introduced short-order cooking to Spain – *madrileño* used to indicate quicker dishes. The city is spoiled for fish and delicatessens. In May, San Isidro is celebrated with mixed salads and puff pastries.

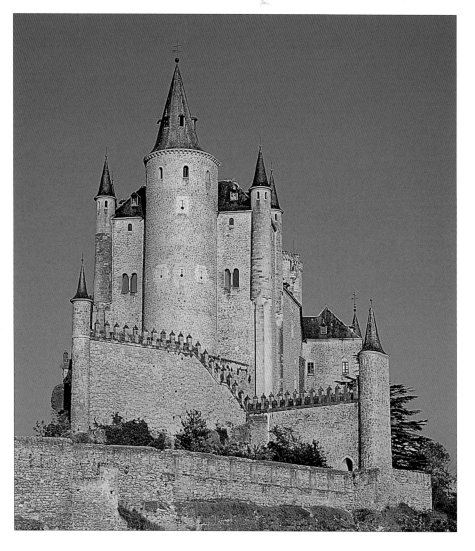

Left: The fairytale Alcázar *(fortress) of Segovia is one of the many medieval castles scattering central Spain – giving the region its name, Castile.*

New Castile and La Mancha

La Mancha, Don Quixote country, means parched. No wonder Cervantes chose it for his poor knight. The great plains are covered with low vines, with odd corners of saffron planted by the Moors. The intense heat of the summer fuels a preference for strong, robust flavours. *Sopa de ajo* (garlic and bread soup) and dishes with cumin are typical fare. Huge quantities of thyme are mixed with pig's liver, paprika and pine nuts, or go into meatballs and one-pot stews.

The food is simple yet quite delicious – glistening tomato salads, luscious *el asadilla* (baked sweet red peppers) and fabulous marinated vegetables such as aubergines (eggplant) pickled in Almalgro in the Moorish fashion. Genuine *pisto* is simply made using (bell) peppers, tomatoes and courgettes (zucchini). Paprika, for red sausages, is made here and in the neighbouring La Vera valley from *choricero* chillies. *Morteruelo* is a liver pâté with game. Best-known of all, however, is *tortilla* – the thick, solid potato and onion omelette. This classic was originally prepared, it is said, by a peasant for a hungry king. Valdepeñas make the best wines, good enough for a *chateo* (a walk round the bars) in Madrid.

Above: Wild black Ibérico pigs forage under the holm oaks of Extremadura, where acorns give their hams special flavour. The region is famous for its pork consumption and its sausages.

Below: In Castile, sheep are valued for their wool and milk, which is turned into cheese. Their meat is eaten while the animals are still young and tender.

Extremadura

The rolling plains are called the *charro* – a land of holm oak and corks, knee-deep in flowers in spring, with more pigs and sheep than people. The explorers Cortes and Pizarro were born here – and left to find something better. Extramadura is poor and there is a good deal of hunting for free food: birds, rabbits, frogs, freshwater fish and summer truffles. Rich tomato sauces are favoured for many of these foods.

Montanchez and Guijelo are famous for *pata negra* (black foot) hams. The black pigs run wild under the oaks, fattening up on acorns. The locals are great consumers of pork. The seasoning of the mince (ground pork) for sausage-making is tested in *prueba* (meatballs). *Pringada* is anything fried in bacon fat. Everything from the pig that can be is made into sausages, and the rest is either pickled, stewed or minced in some manner. The region produces half the pork pâté eaten in Spain.

Migas (fried breadcrumbs) are served with fry-ups, or combined with bacon and chillies. Local hospitality demands that the plates are always piled high. Local paprika colours *el frito* (fried lamb) red; *caldereta extremeña* is lamb stewed with its liver.

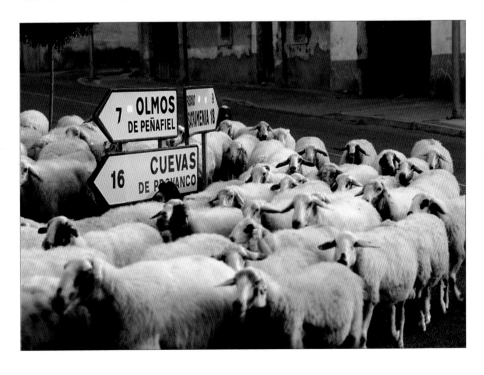

THE NORTH COAST

Isolated from the rest of Spain, the wet north has a rugged coast and a Celtic tradition that links it closely to its northern neighbours.

Galicia

Europe's western corner is green and misty, the chestnut trees rocked by the wind that blows on two coasts. *Hórreos* (stone-roofed storehouses), which are used for storing maize (corn), potatoes and local cheeses, stand guard outside every house.

Below: Vineyards above the Miño River around the village of San Esteban in Galicia produce white wines.

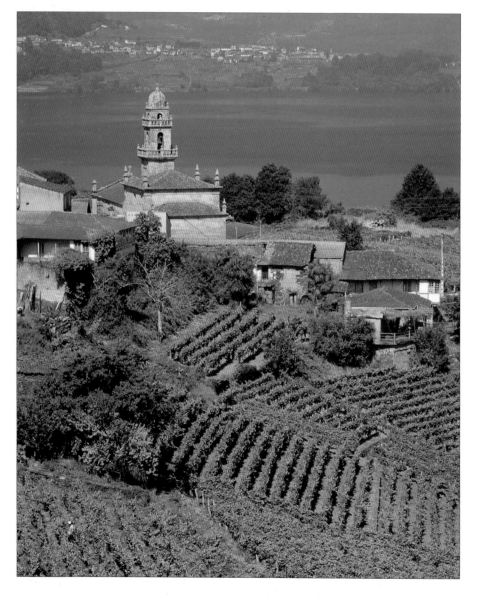

Galicia grows innovative produce for the Madrid markets, including *padrón* peppers, watercress and kiwi fruit. The favourites at home are a special white potato (*cachelo*), which is indispensable for any traditional meal, turnips and, more particularly, *grelos* – the turnip leaves just coming into bud.

The poorer south is covered with chestnut trees, whose nuts were long a basic food but which are now eaten at festivals. Three-quarters of the land provides pasture for dairy cows, whose milk is used to make the famous Galician cheeses such as *tetilla*. Here you will also find the blond breed *rubio gallego*, which supplies much of the country's best meat. Unemployment is rife, however, and the region is called "the goodbye lands" because people leave in the hope of finding a better future in Latin America.

Maize grows on the north coast, and the local breads, heavy in texture, are made with corn meal, barley and rye. Raisins are sometimes added to the corn bread for Christmas.

The Moors never conquered these Celtic lands, which have more in common with Normandy and Wales than they have with provinces further south. Oil and garlic are seldom used in the kitchens of this region and cooking tends to be simple. Fat pigs are prized; the native dish is *lacón*, the salted front leg. Markets sell rolls of back fat for cooking, as well as tripe and numerous types of sausage. Barnyard poultry produce red-yolked eggs, and fat ginger hens are sold with unshed eggs inside.

Cape Finisterre – the world's end and the last stop before America – is known as the Cape of Death, because of the number of ships wrecked there. It provides the best choice and quality of seafood in the world. Half of the mussels eaten in the world grow here.

Windy, westward Santiago de Compostela cathedral, with its cliff-face façade, is a place of world pilgrimage, famous for the grave of St James. The pilgrims' badge is a scallop shell, and even those who do not wear it must surely eat them. Vigo is the biggest fishing port in Europe.

New wineries of gleaming steel make wine from grapes that grow on the south-facing seaside slopes. The white *alberiño* is said to come from a Riesling grape brought by German monks. Its "green" wine is often sparkling – the perfect partner for shellfish.

Galicia has over 200 food festivals a year, celebrated with bagpipes, tambourines and simple dances. An ancient pre-Christian culture lies just beneath the surface, with herbalism and a touch of witchcraft. In the magic ritual of the *queimada*, which is used for divination, a rough brandy (*orujo*) and sugar are flamed. The chief witch, in his straw cape, sets fire to the pot. The lights go down and the flames shoot up.

Above: The stone hórreos *that are used for storing corn cobs and local cheeses can be seen all over Galicia.*

Asturias and Cantabria

The range of mountains that run east to west along the north coast stretch 500km/300 miles, with many peaks at 2,500m/8,000ft. Oak and beechwoods support spectacular wild life – bears, wolves and wild cats, as well as deer, boar and capercaillie. Civilization here dates back to the Bronze Age.

This is "green Spain", with some 250 varieties of apple, and where cider-drinking is a serious sport. Clogs are worn against the frequent drizzle, while cauldrons of stew offer a different form of protection against the cold in this mining country. *Pote asturiana* combines cabbage, beans, salt foreleg, pig fat and ribs. Great melt-in-the-mouth white kidney beans go into *fabada*. In the hinterland of Santander, known as *la montaña*, you will find stews of mutton and beans, as well as the bullet cabbage. There are also bean stews with clams and other shellfish.

All four northern regions are famous for their smoke-cured sausages. The *morcillas* (blood sausages) are dried out, then reydrated in stews. *Botiello* (ribs and tail) are served at carnival.

High up, flower-strewn dairy pastures provide the milk for half of Spain's cheeses. The Picos de Europa have 27 varieties, including the famed *cabrales*. This is a dairy culture, which sends milk and yogurt across Spain; at home the milk and butter are used in rice puddings, apple batter cake and butter sponges for breakfast. The Val de Liébana produces wonderful cheese; it is also an enclave of Mediterranean agriculture, growing tiny, delicious chickpeas as well as fruit.

Oviedo, a centre of coal and iron mining, is a wealthy and fast-living city. It has fabulous seafood such as the *changurro* (spider crab) and many modern creations by talented chefs. This is the largest salmon-producing region in the country. Classically the fish is soaked in milk, salt and lemon, then grilled (broiled) – *a la parrilla.*

Cantabria, the corridor west from the Basque country, is a coast of small bays and little fishing harbours, with the flag-flying casino city of Santander. Sardines are found in abundance and the very popular hake is cooked *a la sidra* (in cider), with mussels and brandy. Squid (*rabas*) are breaded and fried.

Above: Scallop shells are the symbol of St James at Santiago de Compostela. These are painted with his sword.

Below: The Asturias is milk country and the rich pastures that cover the hillsides offer excellent grazing.

ALONG THE PYRENEES

Three very different provinces border France. The successful Basque Country, smaller Navarra and large, poor Aragon.

The Basque country

Snuggled into the Pyrenees by France, el País Vasco has many Michelin-starred restaurants. The lucky Basques have it all; well-hung beef, wild mushrooms, fish and vegetables. Long recognized as Spain's finest cooks, they do things the French way, using butter and cream (unusual for Spain), and take their food very seriously. Basque chefs embraced *la nueva cocina* a quarter of a century ago, seeking a profile that extended beyond Spain.

Eating is thoroughly social, with an eatery per every 1,000 people. The Basques adopted the *pincho* (a *tapa* on a stick) and are sophisticated tapas crawlers. In the *cofradías* (men's clubs), cooking is done by the members, who create dishes with *angulas* (elvers) and *kokotxas* (the tasty part of hake throat).

Basques are nationalists through and through, with their own exotic language. The "TX" of the Basque language can prove tricky. The small glass used for

Below: The Pyrenees offer grazing for Basque sheep, whose milk is made into the richly flavoured cheese, Idiazábal.

Above: Basque fishermen unload their catch at Getaria. The Basques have the largest fishing fleet in Spain.

local wine, *txiquito*, is pronounced *chiquito*. The perfumed spider crab is called *txangurro*, pronounced *changurro*. "TX" over a restaurant door anywhere in Spain means that the chef is Basque, which is usually a good sign.

The Basques have a long connection with the sea, with some of the biggest fleets in the world. Cod is mainly fished off the coast of Iceland, to be sold, salted, in *bacalao* shops. Salt fish goes

into *zurraputuna*, a soup with bread and chilli, and *porrusaldo*, soup with leeks, which is eaten mid-morning as the workmen's breakfast.

Fish from Biscay, the waters of Viscaya, is cooked *a la brasa*, over charcoal. Perfectionists say that fish is only worth eating if it has been line-caught rather than netted.

Basque cuisine boasts four main sauces to serve with fish. White sauce, *pil-pil*, is an emulsion of olive oil and garlic; green *salsa verde* combines wine and parsley and is usually served with hake; *vizcaína* (Biscay) is tomato-based; and the fourth sauce is black, made with the ink of the cuttle fish, and often served with it, *en su tinta*.

Spring brings new peas (*tarvillas*) and beans, eaten with other new shoots in *coussinat*, and fungi stalls at markets. In this maize region, corn meal cakes are made on the griddle. But the locals prefer beans – red, black and all shades between – and sausages.

For dessert there are apples (*reinettas*) and *cañutillas* (cream horns), and this is also Spain's main chocolate centre. Firm cheeses are made around Idiazábal and are slightly caramelized when smoked.

Rioja is known for its style of wine, which is flavoured from storage in oak casks. It is the best known of Spain's wine and most widely drunk abroad.

Navarra

This tiny region is relatively isolated, with one highway, the great Valley of Roncesvalles, once passed through by many millions of pilgrims. These travellers are remembered with *bacalao al arriero*, now often a cream of salt cod and garlic, and a hank of *chistorra* sausage. The cheese of Roncal is firm and widely enjoyed in France. Mountain dishes include mushrooms with herbs, roast quail in fig leaves in September and brown trout. Lamb is fried in *cochifrito* or stewed with red (bell) peppers as *chilindrón*.

The fashionable, fruity wines are red or rosé. The vineyards face those of Rioja across the Ebro, Spain's greatest river. Peppers, asparagus and lettuces also grow well here. The many almonds grown in the region are ground for cake-making and marzipan, which is extremely popular.

Below: Vineyards in Navarra produce strong but very fruity wines.

Aragón

Huge Aragón boasts soaring mountains, with many chamois and boar. Game is a speciality, especially the birds that skim over the mountain passes. Pigeons are served in *salmorejo* (garlic and vinegar sauce) and partridges with chocolate, an idea that has caught on across the country. The hams of Teruel, one of the

Above: Bright yellow sunflowers are grown for their seeds, which are often served as a tapa, *or crushed to make margarine or cooking oil.*

three best in the country, are eaten as *magras con tomate* locally, where slices of ham are served in tomato sauce.

Aragón is sometimes mocked for the simplicity of its cooking – the locals like grills, such as goat on a spit, served with *allioli*. Stews with vegetables, baked dough rounds with sardines and red (bell) peppers, and *migas* (fried breadcrumbs) with chocolate are all popular dishes.

Downwards to the dusty plain, Zaragoza is a large grower of maize (corn), sunflowers and many herbs. Borage is still cultivated and used in the same way as spinach. *Boliches* are white beans of great quality.

Groves of almond trees date from Moorish times, with apple, cherry and peach orchards stretching from Zaragoza to Teruel. Here they make *vi rancios* (fortified dessert wine) and cystallized fruit and candied peels. Delicious almond sweetmeats are a reminder of the long Moorish rule.

THE EAST COAST AND THE ISLANDS

As with the other regions of Spain, the east coast and the islands that lie off the mainland have their own specific culture, flavour and traditions.

Catalonia

The French discovered the excellent fish on the Costa Brava, and named the place the Wild Coast. Ever since then people have travelled to Spain to eat *zarzuela* (fish stew studded with shellfish) and *susquet*, with tomato and potatoes. Gerona is famous for its sea bass, and Barcelona for its monkfish in a dark cream of toasted garlic.

Catalonia, the small province next to France, is the hub of Spain's business and commerce and earns one-fifth of the national income. The cuisine here leans towards the French tradition of fine cooking mixed with a little Italian spontaneity – and less towards Africa.

Sauces are thickened with yolks and béchamel is used. Ducks are reared, and confit and magrets (breast fillets) are on the menu.

Catalans have a long tradition of good restaurants – and are now thought of as Spain's best cooks alongside the Basques. (French chefs voted *El Bulli* to be the world's top restaurant.) Barcelona boasts 10,000 eateries, and its market, *la Boquería*, is one of the world's greatest.

Catalan cooking is eclectic. *Allioli* was invented here and first recorded in AD100. Saffron and the tradition of combining meat with fruit go back to the Roman times. Sweet-and-sour is a Moorish taste, while lobster with chocolate came later. Other dishes are inspired by local ingredients – *mar i muntanya* (sea and mountain) refers to dishes that combine seafood and meat such as clams with partridge. Black rice with squid ink is a modern speciality.

Above: A shop window in Catalonia displays a wonderful selection of foods, including sausages, hams and cheeses.

Almonds, onions, spinach and aubergines (eggplant) remain popular, and the provincial dish is the chickpea *escudella* with pork dumpling, served in two courses. White beans are called *mongetes* here and are cooked with *botifarro*, the local sausage. Vic, a sausage capital, produces a black-and-white speciality, as well as the carmine drumstick, *fuet*.

Quality shows in simple foods such as *pa amb tomàquet* (bread rubbed with garlic, oiled and rubbed with the ripest tomato). There is also the *rovelló* mushroom of autumn, and rich, tangy tomato sauce flavoured with bitter orange peel.

Unlike many homes in Spain, Catalan houses have ovens, and cakes for dessert means puff pastries, sweet *cocas* (like pizzas) and little almond and pine nut cookies. The region is the centre of creative wine-making – and *champán's* biggest house in the world, Cordoníu. There is even a non-drip bottle, in the *porrón*, to drink from.

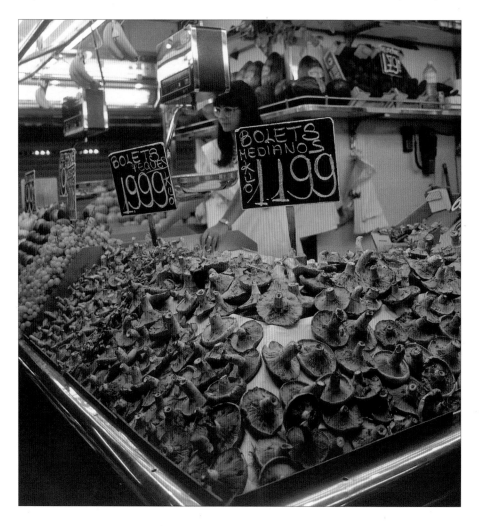

Left: The Boqueria market in the centre of Barcelona sells the freshest seasonal foods such as rovellones *(bleeding milk cap mushrooms).*

The Levante

The east coast includes Alicante and Valencia and a good many of Spain's sunshine beaches. Paella was invented here by picnicking men, and it is still customary to have a *tío* (uncle) in charge. Lake Albufera has freshwater eels, eaten with pepper (*alli-pebre*). Rice dishes often include special runner (green) beans, or *garrafones* (huge flat dried white beans). These are described as "paving stones across rice" in the dish *arros empedrat*.

Alicante's paella contains chicken and rabbit, rather than seafood. Alternatively, it may be made with pasta instead of rice to make *fideuá*. Fresh sausages, *blancs*, are popular, as is the black *poltrona* sausage.

It was a priest who had the brilliant idea of planting oranges commercially here in the 1780s. Now they are on the trees year-round. There are lemons and dates, too, and muscat grapes that survive the heat until after Christmas. *Horchata*, a cool milky drink made from *chufas* (tiger nuts) is a local speciality. It is also a region of festival cakes and Christmas *turrón* (nougat).

Below: The Forn des Teatre bakery in Mallorca is famous for its ensaimadas *– coils of exquisite pastry.*

The Balearic Islands

Mallorca, Menorca and Ibiza are islands with good lobsters and fish, and gulleys full of herbs. The British fleet, which was stationed in Menorca for 150 years, left gin, clover and dairy cows that now provide the milk for the cheese *mahón*. The French discovered *mahonesa* (mayonnaise) here in the 1750s and instantly adopted it.

Above: Fishing boats in the water in Cristianos port, Tenerife, Canary Islands.

Food tends to be solid, as in the layered-vegetable *tumbet*, along with rich soups, and snails from the earthenware *greixonera*. Pigs take centre stage, the high point being the exquisite, spreadable, bright orange *sobrasada* sausage, which is widely available outside the Balearics.

An overlay of cultures has left Moorish-influenced *sucrerías* (sweet shops), which sell jams, pastries and an exquisite cheesecake (*flao*).

The Canary Islands

Las Canarias specialize in local fish, which are beautiful in their varying colours, such as the yellow-purple *vieja*, and cooked simply. They are served with unusual wrinkled potatoes (*papas arrugadas*), which are cooked in sea water and served unpeeled. With them comes *mojo*, a green sauce of blended garlic, coriander (cilantro) and vinegar. A climate of eternal spring produces a wealth of vegetables, including corn. The islands are known for small, sweet aromatic bananas, which are a good partner for the rich, amber *malvasía*, a local dessert wine.

THE SOCIAL CONTEXT

The Spanish are a gregarious people and much of their social life revolves around food. Many people breakfast in a bar before going to work; others go out mid-morning.

They can enjoy *café con leche*, *zumo* (juice) and *tostadas* (toast) or, if they are lucky, a sophisticated roll such as *ensaimada* or *sobao*. For anyone in no hurry, there is always hot chocolate served with *churros* – long strips of deep-fried batter for dunking in the thick chocolate drink.

Lunch is a big affair, typically starting at around two o'clock but later on feast days. The old pattern, in middle-class households, was to eat meat at lunch, then fish at night, with vegetables as a first course. Now it is one or the other. Children have a *merienda* (drink and snack) at about five o'clock. Women often meet friends for a *merienda* after work. Whole families go for the *paseo* – a seven o'clock promenade. Men might go for an *aperativo*. Supper is late, and is a light meal, often vegetable-based.

Large cities never seem to sleep. Dinner bookings are made for ten o'clock at night, and in Madrid there is a rush hour at three in the morning as everyone goes home to sleep before starting work at eight that morning. And the famous siesta? The lunch hour, for office workers, is two hours long and is mainly spent talking.

MENUS

Salad is universal as a first course in summer. Placed in the centre of the table, everyone uses their own fork to eat from it. A restaurant will offer ham or several cold meats, egg dishes, shellfish and soups. The latter are often heavy, and would be regarded as stews elsewhere. Rice and pasta are listed separately, but are a first course in Spain. Then there is a fish or meat course, perhaps offered *a la brasa* or from the *barbacoa* (cooked over charcoal). Restaurants offer desserts, but at home these are usually reserved for saints' days and fiestas.

COOKING AT HOME

The Spanish tradition is for slow-cooking, which can go on all day. The *puchero*, a pot of mixed pulses and meats or sausage, was made most days and left on the stove, wafting rich aromas around the house. Mothers were kept busy in the kitchen but life is different now, and many women work. The delicatessen round the corner stays open until late and supermarkets, with their ready meals, are open all hours.

Left: Cafés provide drinks thoughout the day, offering a place to pause and relax or to meet friends and family.

Table manners
Good children keep their hands on the table throughout a meal, so nothing can go on "underneath the counter". It is thought very bad manners to leave any food on your plate, and anyone not mopping up with bread is considered *mal educado*.

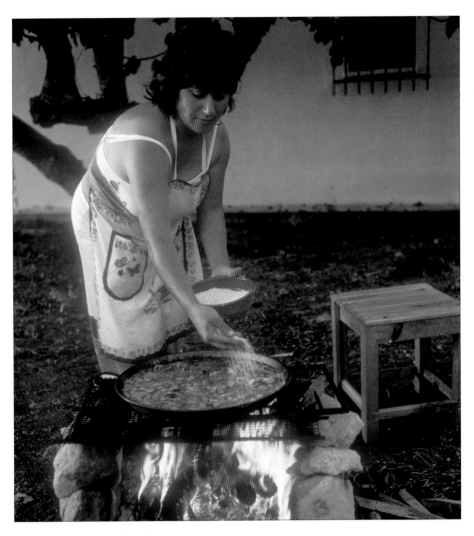

THE GREAT OUTDOORS

Eating outdoors is part of the Spanish psyche and houses have balconies and patios, and perhaps a little outdoor summerhouse called a *comedor* (eating place) because it is often too hot to sit in the sun. Built-in charcoal barbecues grace many gardens.

The Spanish are great picnickers. On casual occasions, family groups may go for a happy day out in the *campo* (fields), or for a harvest picnic. For more formal gatherings such as pilgrimages and fairs, makeshift booths or houses (*casetas*) are put up for entertainment. They offer dining, dance floors and kitchens with gas tripods over which paella is cooked. As many as 2,000 people may be accommodated for the night at unpublicized local events, in tents that are put up and taken down in a single weekend.

Above: Outdoor cooking is a big part of Spanish life and many homes have a built-in fire or barbecue in the garden.

RESTAURANT CULTURE

Families eat out together at weekends, with all the generations present. This is one of the reasons why restaurants are so numerous and prices remain so affordable. Hospitality is offered in restaurants rather than at home and many eating establishments advertise catering for large numbers. Jokingly called a *palacio de boda* (wedding palaces), big parties celebrate not just weddings but First Communions and golden weddings. Spectacularly tiered cakes may appear at any of the celebrations. These large parties are paid for by the guests, who come with large cash rolls: the bill is paid, then the rest forms the bridal gift.

TAPAS

Tapas are Spain's greatest food invention. "Eat when you drink, drink when you eat" is the philosophy.

The idea comes from Andalusia. It started, so they say, with a piece of bread, soon topped with ham or cheese, balanced over a glass, to keep out the flies – the word *tapa* means a cover.

Classic tapas

Tapas dishes revolve around shellfish. In the southern triangle of sherry towns – between Jerez de la Frontera, El Puerto de Santa Maria and Sanlúcar de Barrameda – you may eat amazing shellfish, including squid eggs, whelks (*cañadillas*) and fritters of minute shrimps. The south is also famous for fried fish, *cazón* (a type of shark) marinated in saffron, and *frita malagueña* (mixed battered seafood).

Charcuterie is an important part of the tradition. Hams hang over every bar, with little upturned paper umbrellas underneath to catch melting fat: the incomparable scarlet *jamón serrano*.

Fried tapas in the north evoke an era of nostalgia, with béchamel-based *croquetas* (croquettes), and *gambas en gabardinas* (prawns/shrimp in batter).

Bars are also the place to find local food specialities such as spider crab in San Sebastián, and elvers and hake throats in Bilbao. The morsels can often be very elaborate. Tapas bars are also a wonderful way to sample Spain's best dishes such as *rabo de toro* (bull's tail) and the delicious *escabeche de perdiz* (vinegared partridge).

City specialities

Madrid favours tripe, *boquerones en vinagre* (anchovy fillets cured in vinegar) and, of course, shellfish. The old tradition was to throw prawn and shrimp heads on the floor of the bar to show how popular the place was. In Barcelona, designer bars are all the rage and people go there to see and be seen. Basque bars in cities reflect a much more bourgeois clientele. The phrase *ir de pinchos* means to go for a tapas crawl, which can be a popular way to spend an evening.

FEAST DAYS AND FIESTAS

In Spain, almost every event involves food. There are special foods for feast days – and feast days solely to celebrate food. Every town, and nearly every village, has its fiesta – over 3,000 occur annually. All are occasions for dressing up, parading the children and drinking with the neighbours.

Holy week is an occasion of high drama but the local saint's day, or an incident in a town's history, will be celebrated with processions and street crowds. The seasons of the year are also greeted with affection.

CHRISTMAS AND NEW YEAR

The Christmas lights go up, and there are *belenes* in shop windows, manger scenes often with a huge cast of characters. On Christmas Eve, *Noche Buena*, it is elvers if you are Basque, or perhaps a salt cod cream (*bacalao al arriero*) after midnight mass in Aragón. The Madrid choice is baked *lubina* (sea bream) and red cabbage; the Catalans eat roast turkey. There are gifts of almond *turrón* and marzipan on the table. Twelfth night is a magical day for children; it is the day they receive gifts.

The three kings' arrival in Bethlehem is remembered in the *roscon de reyes*, a crown of rich yeast bread.

On *Noche Vieja* (New Year's Eve), it is grapes at midnight at the Puerta de Sol in Madrid, with costume parties and street festivals in the warmer south. For good luck, people eat one grape for each toll of the midnight bell.

SPRING CARNIVALS

Jueves lardero (Mardi Gras) sees a big carnival in Tenerife, the largest of the Canary Islands. In Andalusia the day is marked with a feast of all good things from the pig, before the start of the 40 meatless days of Lent.

In Valencia, *La Fiesta de Las Fallas* culminates on the saint's day of San José, 19 March. Some 400 huge caricature creations are set alight in one vast bonfire and all-night party. Further south in Alcoy every April, San Jorge is celebrated with a battle reenactment. The saint appears on a white horse to lift the Muslim siege. Black beans with white rice (*moros y cristianos*) are eaten as a reminder.

For Seville's *Feria de Abril*, streets of *casetas* are erected, and days are given over to drinking and dancing. The close is followed by *lunes de la resaca* (hangover Monday).

HOLY WEEK

Semana Santa, the days from Palm Sunday to Easter, is the big festival, particularly in the south. The heavy *pasos* (scenes of Christ's death) and the weeping virgins banked by scented lilies and tall candles are paraded night after night, later and later, before packed crowds and to a constant reverberating noise of drumming.

The Easter foods are few: *torijillos* (fried toast), cheesecake, and perhaps lamb for *Resurreción* day. However, it is *carajillos* (brandy and black coffee) that you will need to cope with the drama and exhaustion of the festival.

Left: The Virgin and Child are paraded around Valencia for the patronal festival. The special relationship of each town to its patron makes her "our" virgin.

Above: The sinister costumes of the penitentes *were adopted in the past to hide the identity of the genuine penitents. Today, they are a traditional part of Holy Week in the south.*

CELEBRATING THE NEW SEASON

Food coming into season is joyfully greeted – the reappearance of freshwater crayfish, the first salmon of the year, a *caracolada* (feast of river snails) in Lerida. Tarragona people wear bibs when they suck the *calçots* (spring onions/scallions) from the barbecued black leaves. In Valls and Cambrils, the celebrations include human towers.

In Murcia, the end of Lent is marked with floats and a parade for the "Burial of the Sardine". The return of sardines to Spanish waters marks the coming of summer. In Malaga, the fish are roasted over beach fires for *la moraga*. Fishermen give thanks on San Pedro and the Virgen de Carmen on 15 July with a flotilla of decorated boats, followed by fish suppers.

For the children
Many festivals start with a carriage procession and a *chupinaza* – pelting children with candy. *Chupa* is a ball of candy on a stick.

SAINTS' DAYS AND PATRONAL FESTIVALS

Spaniards don't have birthdays but instead celebrate their saint's day. For example, if your name is José everyone will remember you on 19 March, with congratulations, flowers and sweets (candy) for the children. It is "your day". Towns, and districts within them, also seek the protection of a saint, whose image is paraded annually. These days are a frenzy of baking.

In Badajoz, people celebrate with little Moorish fritters, and in Logroño they eat yeast buns called *bollas* for San Marco. A topsy-turvy day in Segovia on Santa Agatha, when the men are replaced by "mayoresses", is celebrated by women with moscatel-soaked cake (*ponche segoviana*).

To celebrate San José on 19 March, everyone eats *buñuelos de viento*, little choux puffs that "just blow away". In Madrid these airy pastries are made with lard and *coñac*, and have a special filling of rich, sweet, creamy custard to celebrate San Isidro.

Local cookies come out for fiestas such as the Valencia *Fallas*: baked nut *almendrados*, little *glorias* (pyramids of marzipan and meringue), and sweet pastry *rollets* and *fartons* (fingers of sweet rolled dough, baked and sugared). Santa Clara, patroness of so many nuns, is celebrated in August with *rosquillas* (iced ring doughnuts) and, in the summer, street crowds on the east coast and islands eat *cocas* (flat buns) with candied fruit for St John and St James.

Below: Brightly coloured costumes with a team theme add to the fun at many festivals such as Carnaval *in Cádiz.*

SUMMER IN THE SUN

Summer brings the perfect weather for celebrations. Spain's biggest picnic is *El Rocío* when a million people traipse with wagons, drawn by face-fringed oxen, to the shrine of the *Virgen de Rocío* in Andalusia. The Assumption of the Virgin on 15 August is celebrated with days of street fairs, table tennis, dancing, flirting and flamenco, and is a bigger festival than Christmas. Madrid and Barcelona have year-round festivals, including San Isidro each May in Madrid and Festa de la Mercè every September in Barcelona. All of them serve typical local dishes. Pamplona has the most challenging festival of all from 6–14 July to celebrate San Firmín. Called the *encierro* (bull penning), each day, the bulls chase any who are brave enough to participate across the town.

ST JAMES' DAY – SANTIAGO

Spain's National Day on 25 July means fiesta time in Santiago de Compostela. Jostling crowds of people, many of whom have walked the last few kilometres into town, pack the streets around the cathedral. There are balloons, pavement stalls, music, dancing, fireworks and beauty queens. No one is drunk, just happy. *Gigantes y cabezas* amuse the crowds. The giants (men on stilts) represent figures from the past – Queen Isabel or a Moor. They have comic papier-mâché heads and costumes that go down to the shoes.

To feast on, bars serve octopus *a la feria*, gently stewed with paprika. There is also lobster followed by *tarta de Santiago*, a cinnamon almond tart, with a stencil of St James' great two-handed sword outlined in powdered sugar.

Above: Gigantes *feature in many traditional festivals. Valencia is famous for its papier-mâché figures, which are balanced on the shoulders.*

HARVESTS

In the days when grapes were crushed by men dancing in the vats with bare feet, there was close physical contact to the harvest. Today, abundance is celebrated in a different fashion. *La tomatina*, held in Bunyol in Valencia at the end of August, is the messiest of all these festivals. It starts with trying to get a ham off the top of a greasy pole and is followed by 15 minutes of mayhem as thousands of people pelt each other with ripe tomatoes.

Haro, in La Rioja, celebrates San Pedro at the end of June with a "war of the wines". Neighbours dress up in white and bombard each other with wine squirted from a leather bottle. In the Asturian town of Nava, the cider apple harvest is celebrated by a chain of celebrants pouring cider from pitcher to pitcher down the street. There are plenty of free drinks along the way.

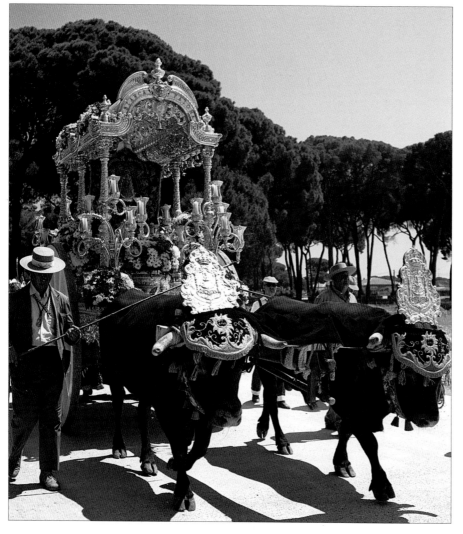

Left: Oxen wearing Cleopatra-style headdresses pull the gilded cart that carries the Virgin of El Rocío on Spain's biggest pilgrimage.

MATANZA – PIG KILLING TIME

The *matanza* is the greatest social festival of the year. The proverb goes: "every pig has his St Martin" (pride comes before a fall), and traditionally 10–11 November is the time for pig killing. If you don't have a pig, then you muscle in on someone else's, because it needs a team for sausage-making. The annual event brings families together and lasts for two or more days. The pig's liver, cooked with onions, is served for lunch on the first day, and the kidneys with rice or potatoes is served on the second.

If you can't find a pig, then you can party at a *matanza* feast in a restaurant, accompanied by oboes, drums and dancing of the *paso doble*. Over 30 courses, the skilled chefs demonstrate just what you can do with a pig. Brains and ears, hot and cold, salad and soup make up the delicious first courses. Hot courses follow: roasts, stews of tail, trotters, marinated loin, roast ham, *solomillo* (tenderloin) with occasional garnishes of vegetables, and tiny roast pigs too. All is accompanied by hunting horns, singing and *olé* to everything.

Above: Dancers skip around a maypole at a local festival in Belunchón, Toledo.

Below: Flamenco dancers at the Fiera de Abril in Seville wear the flounced skirts usually associated with Andalusia. Here, they are known as sevillanas.

THE DAY OF THE DEAD

All Saints, on 1 November, is celebrated by families all over Spain, carrying flowers to the graveyards. *Huesos de santos* (saint's bones), made of almond pastry, sweet potato or batter, are eaten. Sometimes they are fried around a piece of bamboo cane, which makes them ghoulishly hollow. Catalans bake little nut *panellets*. In Galicia, there are all-night vigils by candlelight, with chestnuts roasting on braziers and the mists drifting in from the sea.

CELEBRATION EATING

Huge outdoor meals are a typically Spanish event, but crowd cooking from a single pot is a challenge that only the Spanish would accept. In the town square of Valencia, a vast paella pan 4m/4yds across and set over charcoal was used to cook yellow rice for 1,000 people. The ingredients were stirred with wooden oars.

Vast cauldrons, to dance around as well as to eat from, bubble on fires in the middle of public squares in many places. Arévalo, in Castile, celebrates St John of the Cross in December with a *cocido de San Juan* (plates of beans and chorizo). Benifairó de Les Valls, in Valencia, has its *calderete* of everything porcine, with rice and many vegetables.

COOKING IN SPAIN

The wonderful ingredients of Spain — olives, rice, wine, Mediterranean vegetables, cheeses and sausages, and fish and shellfish from the longest coastline in Europe — have shaped the country's distinctive style of cooking. These fabulous ingredients are matched by the special cooking methods and recipes that best display their virtues.

THE SPANISH KITCHEN

Spanish cooking methods have stayed mainly unchanged over the centuries. Although modern kitchen appliances have taken away some of the labour of food preparation, the pots, pans and techniques remain the same.

COOKING OVER CHARCOAL

This is very much a Spanish tradition. Wood and charcoal fires are still used in homes and many restaurants today. The fire is built on a brick shelf and a metal plate (*la plancha*) sits over the fire at cooking height, with holes for the pots to sit in. It is also used for grilling.

Small terracotta stoves may also be used, heated with charcoal from the main fire in winter, and an outdoor fire in summer. These stoves feature in the 16th-century paintings of Velásquez, and have not changed since that time.

ABOUT THE HOUSE

Spanish winters are chilly, so a *brasero* (two-handled brass tray of hot charcoal) sits under the sitting-room table; a cloth over the table holds in heat, keeping the feet warm. The *brasero* is not actually used for cooking, but is handy for toasting bread.

The cellar (*bodega*) is also of great importance. In the big country *cortijo* (farmhouse complex) the cold cellar stones near the well were often the only cold place. This is where gazpacho was chilled overnight.

Above: Classic earthenware cazuelas *are used for both cooking and serving.*

POTS AND PANS

All over the world the paella pan is identified with Spain. The real Valencian *paellera* has green handles, a dimpled base and is quite thin. They range in size from small to enormous – big enough for a party. The other traditional frying pan is deep and two-handled, used for stews and for deep-frying fish.

The *puchero* (or *olla*) is the pot that has given its name to many Spanish stews. In central Spain it may be earthenware with a bulbous body, narrow neck and two handles but in other areas it is more frequently an upright, loop-handled, metal or copper pot. The witches' kettle (a round-bellied metal *caldereta* with three legs) is used for fish dishes and the rice dish, *arroz caldoso*. A bigger version of this is *un caulderón*, which is used for cooking large stews in public squares at fiestas. It is the classic vessel carried around to Galician fairs by itinerant octopus cookers.

Below: The shallow paella pan and the deep-frying pan are widely used in the Spanish kitchen.

EARTHENWARE DISHES

The earthenware *cazuela* is a splendid invention. Glazed inside, it comes in all sizes from small to very large, and may be rectangular as well as round. In Castile they are used for roasting, and in Catalonia and Levante for oven-baked dishes. Flameproof, when used with a heat diffuser (except over charcoal), the virtue of the *cazuela* is that it retains heat for a long time, but also remains cold, which was crucial in the days before refrigeration.

BOWLS, JARS AND JUGS

There are many traditional bowls and vessels that are still used in kitchens today. *Lebrillos* are earthenware mixing bowls. The *cuenco*, with a small base and straight sides rising to a wide rim, is characteristic, and the large bowl is used in the south. The wooden *artesa* is a trough used for kneading bread and salting hams. Traditional gazpacho bowls are made of olive wood and in the north the saucers used for serving octopus are also wooden.

Storage jars come in many wonderful shapes and sizes and may be lidded or unlidded. Some jars are glazed and painted, while others are simply glazed on the inside. The unglazed *tinaja* is a handleless urn of Moorish origin that is used for storing wine and grain or, in Catalonia, oil. You will see huge ones sitting by the roadside driving south into Valdepeñas.

Below: Small brown casserole dishes cook individual servings.

Above: This earthenware apothecary's jar is a typical type of storage container.

Many modern kitchens have two oil jugs (pitchers) labelled *aceite de pescado* and *aceite de carne* each with its own strainer. The former is used for cooking fish, and the latter for cooking meat. Oil is stored in these jugs after frying for reuse. A popular wedding present is a matching set of oil jugs on a tray, with china vinaigrette bottles and cruets, and a jar for toothpicks.

Below: Traditional gazpacho bowls are made of olive wood.

Traditional drinking jugs

In the Andalusian countryside men go to work carrying a *botijo*, a round pot with a handle and two spouts – one for filling and the other, narrower, one for drinking.

The more elegant Catalan equivalent is the glass *porrón*, which is used for passing hand-to-hand indoors. Its long, thin spout tips into the mouth, but the body of the jug slopes backwards, to prevent spillages.

KITCHEN EQUIPMENT

There are many gadgets in the Spanish kitchen, some for general use and others that are used for a specific dish. Originally, the mortar and pestle were used for the tasks that are now carried out using a food processor or blender. The Spanish *almirez* (mortar), which comes in varying sizes, has four "ears", one of which has a pouring channel. It was introduced to Spain by the Moors and had a huge impact on Spanish cuisine. Dishes such as *salmorejo* (a smooth garlic and tomato soup) became possible, eventually leading to the creation of gazpacho. Purists still press gazpacho through a hair sieve but the mixture can also be pounded or finely chopped. Today, most people chop the vegetables in a *cuenco* (earthenware bowl) using a hand-held blender.

La quemadora is the tool used for caramelizing sugar on *crema catalana* – the metal disc attached to a wooden handle is heated, then held close to the sugared surface to give a caramel finish.

A ridged rolling pin is used to make striped pastry for sweet *empanadillas* (the savoury ones are unstriped) and dariole moulds are used to make *flan* (baked custard). Traditional kitchens also have a box on the wall covered with a cloth, or a drawer in the dresser, for storing stale bread. Bread is bought daily, and eaten with meals. Leftover bread is pounded and used to thicken soups and sauces.

THE OLIVE TREE

One of the oldest cultivated trees, and one of the oldest Mediterranean crops, the olive tree is thought to have been spread throughout Spain by the Phoenicians before 1000BC. Spain is now the largest producer and exporter of olive oil, most of it from the south. These oils are typically rich and fruity, with an olive aroma.

GROWING OLIVES

The Mediterranean basin is defined by where olives will grow. Three-quarters of olive oil comes from the south of Spain, but olives also grow to the west as far north as Madrid and to the Pyrenees at Huesca in the east, with a corridor through La Mancha to Valencia.

Olive trees grow on flat or hilly land, but need winter cold as well as warmth to flourish. They blossom in May in an explosion of white flowers. Half of Spain's olives are the *picual* variety, which turn black on the trees before being picked for oil at the end of November. About 4–5kg/8¾–11lb olives are needed to make a litre of oil.

In Catalonia, oil-making dates back to Roman times, when Spanish oil was a luxury product. The region's favourite tree, the *arbequina*, is small and not particularly vigorous, producing large amounts of small olives that never turn black, even when fully ripe. The oil is smooth and low in astringency with, some say, a slight banana flavour. Catalonia has three *Denominación de Origen* (D.O.) areas (although these represent just 4 per cent of production): Borjas Blancas in Lérida, Siurana west of Tarragona, and Las Garrigues in the southern part of Lérida.

Andalusia has a different oil tradition that dates back to Moorish times. The oil is very fruity, with high astringency. It is made from *picual* with *hojiblanca* (the white-leaf variety of olive). It has a lower oil yield but a fresh taste and strong aroma. The D.O. areas are Córdoba and Jaén: Baena and Priego de Córdoba in the former, and the Sierra de Segura and Sierra Magina in the latter. The Montes de Toledo, Murcia and Aragón also have D.O. areas.

OLIVE OIL

The health benefits of the Mediterranean diet are owed, in part, to olive oil. The oil is rich in oleic acid, which can help to reduce levels of bad cholesterol and raise levels of good cholesterol. It contains vitamin E, a natural oxidant that helps bone formation in the young and old. It also helps reduce blood pressure and may even be an aphrodisiac for women, for it is high in the female hormone oestrogen.

However, it is for its kitchen virtues that the olive has been cultivated. A simple dressing of virgin oil brings out the flavour of food, cold or hot. Olive oil is also the best choice for frying, as the subtle bitterness of Spanish oil counters the rich effect of frying. It can also be used to preserve food – the Moors used

Left: Unfiltered single-olive oils such as this one are new in Spain.

Left: An unfiltered (opalino) extra virgin green olive oil

it for storing fresh beans. The high acidity of Spanish oil makes it ideal for making sauces and emulsions such as mayonnaise, which was first made in Spain.

Once exposed to air, oil deteriorates and should be used within three months, though top-quality oils may keep well for up to a year.

OIL CATEGORIES

Flor de aceite is top of the range – the "flower" of the oil that seeps from the crushed olive paste as it revolves in the barrel. Spain's best oil is clear, golden Nuñez de Prado from Baena. Extra virgin (or cold pressed) is the oil that drips from olives crushed on mats. The difference between extra virgin and virgin is the acidity. Top-quality oils must have less than 0.8 per cent acidity. Spanish oils are always labelled with the acidity and the average is 0.4 to 0.8 per cent (virgin oils may be higher). Unfiltered oils deteriorate more quickly. *Aceite de orujo* is oil extracted chemically from the leftover paste. Branded olive oils (formerly labelled "pure") have about 15 per cent virgin oil added for the flavour. Two well-known Spanish brands are Carbonel and Ybarra.

Denominación de Origen
As with the system for wine, the best olive-producing areas are given D.O. status, and the quality of their products is carefully regulated.

OLIVE OIL SAUCES

Aliñada Virgin oil is often used as a dressing for cooked food. The name literally means embellished.

Ajada This is north coast food. Fish is fried in the oil, then vinegar and paprika are added to make a sauce.

Allioli Garlic and oil are blended to make a thick, white emulsion, which is served with vegetables. The Catalan *allioli amb ous* is allioli with egg yolk, which is served with fish and rice.

Mahonesa Spanish "mayonnaise" takes its name from Mahón in Menorca. It is a rich emulsion of egg yolk and oil and is more subtle than allioli from which it is probably derived. It is the perfect partner for shellfish.

Pil pil Like allioli, this is an emulsified sauce. It combines the gelatine in fish skin with oil. The fish is cooked in the oil, and the oil is then swirled in the hot casserole dish until it thickens.

Making Mahonesa

Put 2 egg yolks in a bowl with a good pinch of salt. Using a hand-held blender, beat well, then add 30ml/2 tbsp vinegar and beat again. Work in up to 250ml/8fl oz/ 1 cup ordinary (not virgin) olive oil, drizzling very slowly at first, until it becomes thick and creamy. Flavour with lemon juice, extra virgin olive oil and pepper to taste.

Above: Negras perlas are fruity black olives with a mild flavour.

TABLE OLIVES

Lawrence Durrell said that the taste of olives is "older than meat, older than wine, a taste as old as cold water". Spain is the world's chief olive producer, with half the crop being exported. The vast majority of these olives grow on unirrigated land within range of Seville.

Spanish cured olives are mainly picked when they are bright green and unripe. At this point, they are low in oil, being made up of only acid and sugars. In this state, the olives will keep their colour and grassy tang for several months after brining. Left on the tree they turn a mottled purple, and finally black, with a softer, fuller flavour. The *muerta* (dead) just drop from the tree, black and wrinkled.

To remove their bitterness, green olives are washed in several changes of water and then stored for a few days in brine (known as the Seville way) with flavourings, to make *aceitunas aliñadas* (seasoned olives). In Andalusia garlic, oregano and herbs are used; in the Balearics wild fennel and lemon leaves. Pitted olives stuffed with little pieces of cooked pimiento, slivers of almond, anchovy or roasted garlic are also sold, and popularly exported.

Left: Allioli made with egg yolks is a powerful garlic mayonnaise with a history dating back over 2,000 years.

Above: Pimiento-stuffed olives were originally filled by hand.

Above: Manzanillas are the best-known and most popular of Spanish olives.

Types of olive

There are many different varieties of olive, each with their own individual appearance and character.

Arbequina comes from the village of La Arbeca in Lérida. It is very small, greenish-brown and has a high oil content and pleasant bitter-to-aromatic flavour. It is *the* Catalan appetizer.

Cornezuelo is horn-shaped, green and with a white tip. It has a strong flavour with a hint of bitterness.

Cuquillo is round, small, and blue-black. It is often prepared with chopped onion and hot spices, and is good as a partner to beer.

Gordal or **reina** (queen) are trade names for the largest, dark green, fleshy olive, often called *sevilles* in Spain.

Hojiblanco is slightly rectangular in shape. One of the main types of olives, it is more fibrous and less tasty than other varieties.

Manzanilla is apple- or pear-shaped, the best-known and most popular olive. It is suitable for stuffing.

Pelotín from Andalusia is small, round and green.

Negra is black, spiced or dried and pickled, and perfect with red wine. Large negras are called *negras perlas*.

CHEESE AND DAIRY PRODUCE

Spain produces about 200 varieties of cheese (*queso*), most of them in farmhouse dairies and with limited distribution. A considerable number are exported, with the hard cheeses being the most successful.

Cheeses are shaped according to local tradition. Muslin (cheesecloth) is used to shape the Galician *tetilla* and also *Mahón*, producing very different results. *Camerano* is a ball-shaped cheese, moulded in a basket. Sycamore or maple leaves are pressed on to the wet rind of northern blue cheeses. Esparto grass hoops give Manchego cheese a welt, which becomes broader on the rind of the *Ronda*.

Although goat's, cow's and ewe's milk all produce distinct cheeses with their own unique character, some generic cheeses are made with milk blends. The semi-hard *Aragón* is made with ewe's and goat's milk, as is *Gamonedo*. Some cheese is smoked – most notably the versions of *San Simón*, *Gamonedo* and *Idiazábal*. *Quesucos* (part of the Liébana D.O.) is a mild, smoked, mixed-milk cheese from Santander, pale yellow inside, with "eyes".

Hard cheeses are often served as a tapas dish, while soft ones are served with honey and nuts as dessert. There is little in the way of cheese cooking – only fried hard-cheese cubes, and *flamenquines* (ham and cheese rolls that are breadcrumbed and deep-fried).

Below: Menorcan Mahón is made using cow's milk. Its bright orange rind is produced by rubbing the rind with butter, paprika and oil.

Right: San Simón is a semi-soft cow's milk cheese from Galicia. It has a supple texture and is often smoked.

FRESH AND SOFT CHEESES

Fresh curd cheese (*requesón*) is much liked and made all over Spain. Ewe's milk is normally used to make matured cheese, but there are some soft ones, which include the white *Anso*, from the valley of Huesca; and the mild *Cervera* and *Puzol*, both from Valencia. Two are widely available and typical: *Queso de Burgos* is rindless, often with mould markings, and soft. It is made from scalded curd, which is moulded then salted in brine for 24 hours. *Villalón* or *pata de mulo*, from the Valladolid region, is an elongated cylinder.

GOAT'S MILK CHEESES

In the south, cheeses are predominantly made with goat's milk. Often pressed, their flavour is distinct and clean. They are not pungent like many of the French varieties, and they have a light, crumbly texture. Unaged goat's milk cheeses include *Alicante*, *Camerano* from the Rioja area, and the slightly aromatic *Málaga*, with its buff rind, lightly pressed into an esparto grass mould. Southern goat's cheeses include: *Cádiz*, which is medium-pressed, full of holes, and with a rind marked with esparto; and *Añejo de cabra* from the *Sierra de Huelva*, whose ripened paste is dark orange, with a rough rind. The Canary Islands make only goat's

cheese, the best being *Majorero*, which is matured for two months. In the east, *Garroxta* is made all over Catalonia. In central Spain, *Ibores* from Extremadura, is made from *retinto* goat's milk. It is aromatic, slightly sour, with a soft oiled rind coated with paprika. *Soría* has a firm white skin and is lightly salted. *Cabra de Tiétar*, from Ávila, is lightly pressed and briefly matured. *Valdeteja*, from León, has a sharp, goaty smell. It is shaped into a cylinder, has some holes and a crusty rind.

COW'S MILK CHEESES

In the north, the cheeses are made with cow's milk. They are generally eaten quite young and are creamy and soft.

Tetilla, from Pontevedra in Galicia, is white inside, moulded with a cloth and sometimes has a golden rind. Its name literally means teat or nipple, reflecting the shape of the cheese. *Cebrero* (*Piedrafita*), from the mountains of Lugo, looks like a chef's hat; it is tangy and white inside. The mild, yellow *Gallego* (*Ulloa*) is a slightly flattened ball. *León* is a yellow drum, with a close texture and rough yellow rind. The dry, astringent *afuega el pitu*, from Asturias, is shaped in a small cone. *Pasiego prensado*, which is made south-west of Santander, is white and creamy with small holes and a distinctive flavour.

Eggs
Spain is a country of poultry breeders and the use of eggs (*huevos*) in cooking reflects this. Galician free-range (farm-fresh) eggs are famous for the deep colour of their yolks – they are used in Madrid for making tortillas.

Menus still have an egg course and proper attention is given to egg cooking. *Revuelta*, soft scrambled eggs, is the way to display such luxuries as summer truffles and caviars. Eggs make everyday meals with a good deal of spontaneity, such as flamenco eggs and other gypsy recipes.

Above:
Idiazábal D.O. has been made for centuries by shepherds in the Urbia and Alara mountains.

San Simón, from the Lugo province in Galicia, is large, shiny, brown and pear-shaped; it is oiled on the outside then smoked, but remains creamy inside.

Extremadura produces two soft-rind, creamy cheeses that are unusual for Spain. *La Serena* D.O., made in Cáceres, and *torta de Casar* are spring cheeses – the latter set with cardoon, which makes it pleasantly bitter. It is very creamy and is usually spooned out of its pink rind.

In the Balearics *Mahón* D.O., from Menorca, owes its existence to the British, who brought Friesian cows to the island, where the salty grazing affects the cheese's taste. It is hand-pressed into rectangles.

BLUE CHEESES

Cabrales D.O. is a real gourmet cheese made from cow's milk (or sometimes a blend) in 25 × 20cm/10 × 8in drums. A worthy competitor to Roquefort, the paste is off-white with blue veins, slightly stonger and more acidic than the French cheese. It is moulded, dry-salted, then matured for about six months in natural limestone caves in the Asturias, then wrapped in plane tree leaves. Related cheeses are *Picón* (part of the *Liébana* D.O.) and *Tresviso*. *Gamonedo*, another Asturian blue made from blended milk, is unusual both for being smoked for ten to twelve days before maturing, and for its wrapping of fern leaves. The white flesh is blue-veined with oval eyes.

SHEEP'S MILK CHEESES

In central-north Spain, Castile and León produce most of the sheep's milk. This is the home of hard, pressed cheeses with dark rinds. Made in big drums, they are well-matured, strong, dense and grainy. *Roncal* was Spain's first D.O. cheese. The ivory paste has tiny holes. *Idiazábal* D.O., from the Basque Provinces, is a classic, holey, often smoked cheese. *Zamorano* D.O., from western Castile, is unpasteurized, made from the best milk in Spain.

Other firm cheeses include *Grazalema* from Cadiz, *Orduña* from Navarra, the *Oropesa* from Toledo and Basque *Gorbea*, with a dark shiny rind, flat base and rounded top. *Pedroches* from Córdoba is piquant and salty, which is brought out by storing it in oil.

MILK

Spain's dairy region is the Cantabrian range, along the north coast. Here cows move up to summer pastures in the high mountains. The Spanish drink milk at breakfast time, mixed half and half with coffee. Fresh milk is drunk by children and the elderly or made into *cuajada* (a sort of junket) and yogurt. Milk puddings have always been popular, and whipped cream (*nata*) is often piped over desserts.

BUTTER

Called *mantequilla*, butter is used for frying in the Basque country. This is one important way Basque cooking can be distinguished from the rest of Spain. Their sauces and cakes contain butter, as they now do in Catalonia. Elsewhere, oil and pork fat still dominate.

All about Manchego

Spain's premier cheese is made from the milk of Manchega ewes from the centre of the country. It is made in 3kg/6½lb drums, or occasionally smaller. Sometimes pasteurized, the curds are heated and pressed into esparto grass moulds, which pattern the outside of the cheese. Golden inside, Manchego becomes stronger as it ages and is sold as *semi-curado* (under 13 weeks), *curado* (up to six months), *viejo* (over six months), and also packed in oil. Mature (sharp) cheeses are similar to Parmesan. Exported cheeses, called *ibéricos* are often made using blended milk.

Below: Manchego, from left, aged for 4 months, 6 months and 10 months.

VEGETABLES OF THE OLD WORLD

The Spanish really appreciate fresh vegetables and a wide range originating in Europe and North Africa are grown there. In spring, fresh peas, the first asparagus and young shoots of garlic are gathered and served in egg dishes and *menestras* (vegetable stews), where their virtues shine. New small artichokes (*alcachofas*) are grilled on the first barbecues of summer.

Growing delicate green asparagus (*espárragos*) is a big industry in the valleys around Granada, while white asparagus are grown in the valley of the Ebro, in Navarre, and canned for sale all over Europe. Other excellent food crops grow there too, including *cogollos* (Little Gem, or Bibb, lettuces). Unusual vegetables such as borage, blue-flowered and hairy stemmed, are still stewed in Aragón. Carrots are another ancient vegetable and flourish in the Spanish sunshine.

Spinach was introduced by the Moors and their *espinacas a la catalana*, with pine nuts and raisins, is still made today. In the south, chard is used in place of spinach (*acelga*), with similar but coarser leaves. The pearly stalks can be battered and fried.

The true vegetable of the Islamic lands is *berenjena*, the aubergine or eggplant (*albergenies* in Catalan). Many recipes using aubergine go back 800 years. *Almodrote* combines aubergine with garlic, cumin, pine nuts and cheese; *alboronia* is similar to ratatouille, but with no tomatoes.

Above: Large Spanish onions are sweet and mild enough to eat raw.

ONIONS AND GARLIC

The Moors loved onions, especially raw, which is one reason why the Spanish onion is so big and mild. *Sofrito* is the combination of onion and garlic fried together to form the base of numerous sauces. *Cebollones* (*calçots* in Catalan) are oversized spring onions (scallions), with the mild flavour of shallots. Young garlic shoots, plucked when green, are similar and these *ajetes* have a spring cuisine of their own, usually cooked with eggs and seafood. Leeks are popular with the Basques and are used in soups such as *purrusalda*.

Garlic is as old as the Pyramids and in Spain many sauces contain this pungent vegetable. *Ajo-pollo*, which means "the sort of sauce used for chicken", combines crushed garlic with ground almonds and breadcrumbs. Valencian *alli-pebre* is a mixture of garlic and paprika, and *alli oli* is simply a mixture of garlic and oil – the names say it all.

Left: Leafy green spinach has been eaten in Spain for centuries and is used in many Catalan dishes.

All about garlic

Fundamental to Spanish cooking, garlic is often mistakenly thought to dominate it. Its role in the kitchen is reflected in the saying, *estar en el ajo* (to be in the know). Garlic is more than a flavouring – it is good for you too. It lowers cholesterol levels and acts as an antiseptic on cuts. It is said in Spain that garlic gives you guts. After the San Fermín bull running at Pamplona, young men take home strings of garlic to build up their courage for the next year.

Used raw or cooked, garlic has two quite different flavours, the first pungent, the second more suggestive. Any dish *al ajillo* is flavoured with chopped garlic, while *con ajo* means "with whole cloves", which are made sweet and mild with long cooking.

In Spanish cooking, garlic is often the first ingredient into the frying pan. It is used to flavour the oil, but is then discarded before the rest of the ingredients are added. Before adding garlic to an uncooked sauce, make a paste by crushing it with a little salt using the flat side of a knife.

Below: Garlic is widely used in Spanish cooking, adding a distinctive flavour.

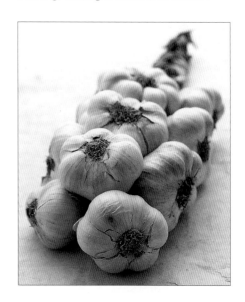

CABBAGES, TURNIPS AND CARDOONS

Galician cabbages are huge, but every province likes this vegetable. There are more words for cabbage in Spanish than in English, and more varieties. *Lombardo* (red cabbage) is popular in Madrid and is used to garnish sea bream on Christmas Eve; a *cocido de berza* will contain cabbage. However, it is turnips that Galicians really love, both the root and the green tops (*grelos*) when they just start budding. Cardoon (*cardo*) is the artichoke's bigger cousin and comes into season at the end of the year.

WILD FOOD

Much produce is gathered from the countryside, especially in poorer areas. Lupin seed is a yellow tapas bar nibble, and is sold at fairs as a snack. Wild asparagus is a speciality, picked in April and again before winter. *Targina* is a thistle with short side stems that are eaten in the same way as cardoon or with beans or eggs. Dandelion leaves go into salads, chicory root is dug to make coffee, and fennel is used to season fish. Chestnuts grow in the south of Galicia and were a basic foodstuff until potatoes arrived.

Capers originally grew wild all over the southern coasts. But they are now a huge industry. Both the buds and the plump berries are pickled, the latter eaten in the same way as olives.

Above: Fresh young turnips and their leafy green tops are Galicia's pride.

WILD MUSHROOMS

The Spanish in general are not great mushrooms pickers, and the Galicians are positively against it. However, the Basques and Catalans make up for this. About 50 kinds of mushroom are gathered throughout the year. They are cooked simply, with garlic or eggs, and are used in game casseroles. Ceps (*bolets*) are grilled (broiled) whole.

Setas (wild mushrooms) and *hongos* (fungi) are much in demand, as are *setas de cardo* (oyster mushrooms). In Catalonia, picking the golden yellow *rovolló* is almost an obsession. Called *níscalo* in the rest of Spain, the bleeding milk cap oozes red drops from the stem when it is cut.

The Basque favourite is the tiny yellowish white spring St George's mushroom with its penetrating perfume. Called *zizak* locally, it is *moixernons* elsewhere. Truffles also grow in Spain, and the common *criadillas de tierra* are served in tapas bars in Extremadura during the summer months.

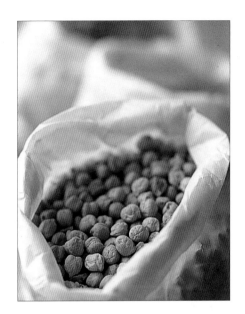

Above: Chickpeas, with their lovely, nutty flavour, are the basic carbohydrate of Spanish cuisine.

DRIED BEANS, LENTILS AND PEAS

Dried broad (fava) beans were used widely in Spanish dishes in years past, and are still used in a few dishes today, such as the Valencian *micherones* (stewed with garlic). Dried peas and lentils (*lentejas*) are still weekly fare, partnered with the inevitable chorizo, particularly north of Madrid.

Chickpeas (*garbanzos*) are the potatoes of Spain, growing well through the hot summers. In ancient times, the Romans mocked the chickpea-eating Spanish, suggesting that their enormous consumption of the legume not only indicated stupidity but also induced it. Chickpeas are the least easy of dried beans and peas to spoil, but do not absorb flavour from accompanying ingredients in the way that beans do. Although they need soaking and take up to 2 hours to cook, chickpeas keep their shape well, even when reheated. *Garbanzos con chorizos* (chickpeas with chorizo) is a classic, while chickpeas, chard and salt cod are combined to make a traditional Lenten dish.

Right: Today, fresh broad beans are far more widely used than dried ones, and are celebrated in a national dish, habas con jamón, *with ham.*

VEGETABLES FROM AMERICA

The colour, sweetness and piquancy of American vegetables, brought home by Christopher Columbus, revolutionized Spanish cooking – and with it, Europe. The Mediterranean climate is ideal for tomatoes, peppers, courgettes (zucchini) and pumpkins. Maize (corn) was adopted in northern Spain, for fattening poultry and as corn meal for bread, and potatoes had their biggest Spanish success fried as *patatas fritas*.

TOMATOES

Today, tomatoes are a great success story in Spain. Three or even four crops a year are produced in the *invernadores* (plastic tunnels) of Almería, and they are loaded into lorries that roar north from southern Spain.

The name *tomate* comes from the Aztec *tomatl*, meaning something plump. The tomato was not an instant success when it was introduced to Spain and was, at first, used simply as the liquid for serving chilli. Tomato sauce was still a novelty as late as the 1820s – and regarded by outsiders as a Spanish curiosity. A *sauce espagnole* in a restaurant in France is a classic meat-stock sauce with tomato in it.

Today tomatoes are combined with sweet (bell) peppers in a huge number of dishes: *gazpacho, pisto, bacalo a la viscaína* (salt cod baked with tomato) and all the dishes called *samfaína*. Tomatoes are sold in two classes: ripest and ripe. The first are for sauces, the second for salads. There are even salads where one tomato is dressed with the juice of another – *ajotomate*.

FRESH PEPPERS

Morrones (bell) peppers, are often two-fist size, fleshy with tough skin, green or the sweeter red. There are other sweet varieties and a long, thin, green one with a thin skin. When soft and baked, red pepper has become an ingredient in its own right, called *pimiento*.

The red *piquillo*, grown in Navarra and Rioja, is the gourmet's pepper. Smaller, stocky and with a point at one end, it is crisper and distinctly piquant. It is often stuffed with cod and baked. It is also wonderful canned, after being roasted over beechwood.

Below: Tomatoes are used subtlely in Spanish cuisine, partnering but never dominating other flavours.

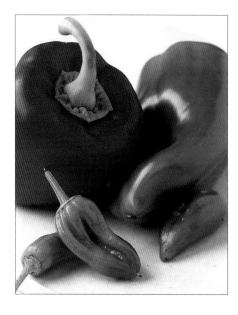

Above: Sweet pimientos *peppers go into many dishes. Little* padróns *are a Galician speciality, popular everywhere.*

The green Galician pepper, *padrón*, is part of a popular joke. As long as a thumb, they are deep-fried and served with a little salt as an appetizer, about twenty to a plate. Though normally sweet, one in that number will be fiery hot, and there is no knowing which.

DRIED CHILLIES

Columbus' mission was to look for the spice, black pepper. He discovered spicy red peppers instead. Towards winter, chilli peppers are hung up all over Spain to dry, particularly in Rioja, in red *ristras* (strings).

The general rule for these chillies is the larger, the milder. Cooking, in particular roasting, makes them sweeter, as the bitterness is in the skin. The flavour of chillies is made more concentrated and robust by drying or toasting. Including vinegar in the recipe gives the same intensified effect.

Choricero This chilli has given its name, colour and piquancy to the red Spanish frying sausage. The chilli is larger than a fist, elongated but rounded, red, and extremely sweet and mild – 1/10 on the Mexican chilli-heat scale. It can be crumbled into dishes or reconstituted in liquid, then the flesh scraped out. One or two per person go into dishes such

Below: Romesco *or* ñora *chillies are usually hung up to dry in long, decorative strings.*

Right: Red kidney beans are a Basque favourite stewed with ham bone, red chorizo sausage and black morcilla.

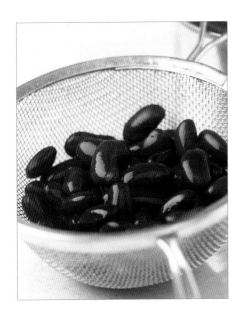

as *chilindrón*, (lamb with chilli).

Ñora This is called *romesco* in Catalonia and is a walnut-sized chilli; red and cherry-round. It has a sweet fruit flavour, with a hint of a biting finish – 2/10 on the Mexican chilli-heat scale. It was adopted by the Catalans in the 16th century and is common in Alicante and Murcia. It has very little flesh but the colour and flavour are concentrated, hence its use in salsas, *romescos* of fish, rice and paella. Ancho or jalapeño chillies may be used as substitutes.

Guindilla As long as a finger, this is Spain's hot chilli – 3/10 on the Mexican chilli-heat scale – but it is also medium sweet. It adds zip to dishes such as *gambas pil pil* (prawns with chilli).

BEANS

Large American kidney beans were considered much more elegant and tasty than old, brown beans. *Judias* are green beans (pods) and *alubias* are dried ones. The latter come in all sizes – from the tiniest *arroncini* (rice-sized) to the big *judiones* of El Barco de Ávila and the *garrafones* (carboys) of Valencia – and in all colours: white, to mottled red or green, to purple with green eyes. Spain is the bean capital of the world.

Every province soon adopted and grew their own beans, in fierce regional competition, cooking them with their own sausages. The Basques once specialized in red beans, but now theirs is the "black" bean of Tolosa. The finest beans grown are *fabes de la granja* from Asturias, used to make *fabada*.

They are very expensive and sold in numbered cotton bags.

Fresh beans make one national dish, eaten with ham, while *pochas* (kidney beans fresh from the pod) are a little October speciality, stewed with quail. A Spanish type that is just becoming known elsewhere is *ferraura*. Bred from runner beans, they are "flat beans", long, soft-surfaced, stringless green pods – and one of the original ingredients of paella.

POTATOES AND SQUASH

While potatoes were ignored in northern Europe, they were a success in Seville. They found their true home in Galicia, which now grows *cachelos*, a large white tuber of exceptional quality, near the sea, where it absorbs salt from the soil. They accompany the local *lacón* (cured pork shoulder) or sardines, and are often layered into fish stews.

Sweet potatoes are *batata* (yellow-fleshed; the US yam) and *boniato* (white-fleshed). They are made into little cakes or served in honey.

The *calabaza* (marrow/large zucchini, summer squash or pumpkins) goes into stewpots like *calabazote* (with potatoes and beans). But *calabacín* (courgette/ zucchini) was little known until the 1980s, and more of a success in Italy.

Below: In the south, squash are added to gypsy vegetable and bean stews.

SPICES, HERBS AND FLAVOURINGS

The Spanish cuisine has its own range of spices, herbs, condiments and nuts, all of which contribute to the unique and characteristic taste of Spanish food.

SAFFRON

With its aromatic scent and golden colour, *azafrán* is a quintessentially Moorish spice. For paella and fish and shellfish stews, there is no substitute. For chicken, all *pepitorias* (nut sauces), creams, buns and ices, saffron is king.

The purple crocuses from which saffron is obtained flower quite suddenly in mid-October in parched La Mancha, creating purple carpets around the vines. The flowers are plucked by hand, then three orange stamens are pulled from each flower, toasted over charcoal and dried to bring out the flavour. A hard day's work produces only about 50g/2oz saffron.

Mancha selecto is the world's best saffron; it is deep red, with long threads and a high oil content. Spain produces 70 per cent of the world's saffron. Although very expensive, a tiny amount flavours a dish for two to three people.

Spanish saffron is rarely powdered, as this is too easy to adulterate with cheap yellow dyes such as safflower (*cártamo*), colouring (*colorante*), and the chemical tartrazine.

Below: Top quality saffron all comes from Spain, grown in La Mancha.

Above: Warm, spicy, aromatic cumin is a legacy of the Moors and is widely used in southern cooking.

OTHER SPICES

The Moors introduced cumin (*comino*) to Spain and it is widely used with vegetables and tomatoes, and with skewered meats. Coriander seeds (*cilantro*) also came from North Africa, and are often partnered with cumin and used to flavour skewered meat cooked on the barbecue. Coloured yellow with turmeric, pork cubes are sold ready-spiced in many southern butchers. Other popular spice flavourings include turmeric (*cúrcuma*), cloves (*clavos*), cardamom (*cardamoma*) and – to a lesser extent – ginger (*jengibre*).

The Catalans are generous users of black pepper (*pimienta*), whereas the rest of Spain uses paprika (*pimentón*).

There is no clear division between sweet and savoury spices in Spain – another Moorish legacy. Nutmeg (*nuez moscada*) goes into *morcillas* (black pudding/blood sausage) – along with cumin, cinnamon (*canela*) and aniseed (*matalhuva*) – and also flavours custards. Cinnamon is the obligatory flavouring used in rice milk puddings and the ice cream that accompanies fruit. It is also commonly used with poultry and in stews, which also often contain saffron.

Aniseed (*anís*) is a key flavour in Spanish food and drink. It is basic to many liqueurs and its seeds are ground and used in many pastries, doughs and sausages. Another very Spanish flavour is dried orange peel (*cachorreña*), which is pounded and added to shellfish and fish soups.

SALT

Intimately tied to Spain's commercial history, the salt trade is an old one, and grew up around the Mediterranean salt pans. Cadiz supplied salt beef for the ships journeying to the Americas, and the Basques have been shipping home salt cod since the 17th century.

Today salt has changed from being a preservative to being a preference. The Spanish seek out foods that contain salt, especially cured foods such as *mohama*, *cecina*, *anchoas* and *botargo* (tuna, beef, anchovies and grey mullet caviar). Salt adds interest to beans, while eating salt fish on Fridays is a 500-year-old tradition.

Paprika

Pimentón is a basic flavouring in Spanish cooking, used like black pepper, and not just sprinkled for decoration. It is made from a sweet red (bell) pepper with a round body and pointed end. There are three grades of paprika used in Spain: *dulce* (mild), *picante* (which contains a little *guindilla* chilli), and *agridulce* (bittersweet). You can substitute cayenne pepper for *picante*. The main centre of production is the Vera valley, where peppers are smoked before being ground.

Below: Sweet paprika is Spain's most commonly used pepper.

HERBS

Bay leaves (*hojas de laurel*) Partnered with rosemary and thyme, aromatic bay leaves make up Spain's herbal trinity. The leaves are added to stews and thrown on the barbecue. Fresh leaves are battered, fried and sugared to make sweet *paparejotes*.

Coriander (*cilantro*) Pungent fresh coriander leaves are thought of as the Portuguese herb and only used in Extremadura and the Canary Islands, where the herb is crushed to make the green *mojo verde* sauce for fish. It is also excellent rubbed over pork to flavour the meat before roasting.

Fennel (*hinojo*) This beautiful herb has a slight flavour of aniseed and grows wild everywhere. It is used to flavour the cooking water for shellfish and its tiny aromatic seeds are sometimes added to home-cured olives.

Lemon verbena (*hierba luisa*) Used to make a delicious fragrant tea, this popular herb can be found growing in many Spanish gardens.

Mint (*menta*) Known as *hierba buena*, the good herb, Moroccan mint is a favourite garden plant. It goes into *morcilla* (black pudding) and is used with offal. *Poleo* is Pennyroyal mint (*Mentha pulegium*), which is used for tea – and also in a soup for hangovers.

Oregano (*origano*) This is the sausage herb, and also goes into meat stews and marinades. Its essential oil doesn't deteriorate with long cooking, so it is one of the few herbs that can be added early on in cooking. The related English herb, marjoram (*mejorana*), is thought of as a medicinal herb in Spain.

Left: Many varieties of thyme grow in the Spanish sierras.

Parsley (*perejil*, or *julivert* in Catalan) The Spanish grow flat leaf parsley, which is milder than curly parsley. It is a popular herb and is used lavishly in Murcia.

Rosemary (*romero*) Snails eat rosemary, so they are used as "rosemary cubes" to flavour rabbit stews and paella. Big old bushes of the wild herb are also used to fuel bread ovens and wood-burning stoves. Rosemary with thyme and chilli are traditionally used to flavour dried bean dishes.

Thyme (*tomillo*) There are several varieties of thyme with small white flowers, which are used for cooking. *Tomillo salsero* (sauce thyme) is picked in April to give to friends at Christmas. The herb is much used to flavour rabbit and, with summer savory (*ajedrea blanca*), to flavour dried bean dishes.

NUTS

Almonds (*almendras*) These are second only to oranges as a major crop. There are two types. The first is the smaller, bitter almond, which is grown only for almond oil and essence (extract), as it is poisonous if eaten raw. The second type is the sweet *Jordan* almond. Of Spanish origin, its name is a corruption of *jardín* meaning garden. Grown in the south-east, they are long, flat and slender, and the best cocktail almonds in the world. *Marcona* almonds are used to make turrón (*nougat*).

Ground almonds are used in place of flour to thicken sauces in Spain. They are the base of *picada*, which thickens sauces instead of a roux, and any dish called a *pepitoria*. Almonds are also pounded for soups, used in biscuits (cookies) and coated with sugar to make festival *almendras garipinadas* and Catalan *ametlles*.

Hazelnuts (*avellanas*) These nuts grow in mountain regions and were farmed in Tarragona, where they are made into a soup. The Basques use them to thicken stews, and they are added to meringues as far apart as Granada and Asturias.

Pine nuts (*piñones*) These come from the cones of the stone pine, one of the West's ancient fertility symbols. The cones are gathered in winter and are then dried through the next summer. The tiny creamy nuts have a slightly astringent taste and are improved by toasting, which brings out and enhances their flavour. They are good used in salads and sauces, or baked in little cakes, such as festival *paneletts* and nut-covered *piñonates*.

Below: Pine nuts have a distinctive taste and are frequently toasted before being added to dishes.

Below: Hazelnuts are used to flavour sweet dishes such as desserts, cakes and cookies, as well as savoury sauces.

RICE AND PASTA

These two staples are at the heart of both everyday family meals and classic celebration dishes in Spain.

RICE

Valencia is forever linked with rice. The Moors planted rice there and it was the only crop that could be grown on the hot Mediterranean littoral in summer.

Rice is eaten daily in the east and south of Spain. It is eaten plain, added to soupy stews, and combined with beans to make stuffings for vegetables. Many *morcillas* (black puddings/blood sausages) contain rice, especially those made in Burgos, Aragón, Rioja and the Levante. *Arroz con leche* (rice pudding) rivals *flan* (baked custard) as Spain's national dessert.

It is the quality and flavour of rice that matters, so flavourings tend to be simple – a pinch of saffron, perhaps with a little bacon and *morcilla* (black pudding). Alicante *arros amb costra*, a Catalan oven-baked dish, comes with a rice crust concealing the chickpea and sausage stew. *Arros perdiu* (partridge rice) is "trick dish" made for Lent – instead of partridge, it has a whole baked garlic bulb in the centre. Valencian restaurants feature a different rice every day, but the popular choice for Sundays is rice with salt cod.

Below: Bomba is the most readily available variety of paella rice.

Above: Paella, originally from Valencia, is probably Spain's most famous dish. It is eaten for celebrations but is also an incredibly popular dish for tourists.

Short grain rice

The short, fat Spanish grain originates from Japanese round rice, rather than the Indian long grain, and it has a slight bite, like risotto rice. Spain became Europe's largest rice producer because it was the first country to try to find a suitable grain for the Mediterranean climate. A large amount of rice is grown in the Seville area but the best type of rice is *Calasparra*, which grows in Murcia. The grains swell dramatically when cooked in stock, absorbing three or four times their volume of liquid.

Below: The prized Calasparra *rice is sold in numbered cotton bags.*

Rice pans and dishes

When cooking rice, there are different types of pan for cooking specific dishes. Paella is cooked in the shallow *paellera*. The Valencian model is thin with a dimpled base. The finished dish should be "dry" (but moist), with every grain separate. Strictly speaking, paella is the Valencian name for the dish, and similar dishes elsewhere should simply be called *arroz* (*arros* in Catalan).

"Wet" rice dishes are soupy and eaten with a spoon. They are often fish dishes, cooked in a round-based cooking pot known as a *caldereta*. The pot gives its name to some of the classic wet rice dishes, including *el caldero* (rice with fish). *Arroz a banda* is rice cooked in fish stock, but separately from the fish (which makes another course). It is the perfect dish to reveal just how good plain rice can be, done the Spanish way. These soupy dishes used to be considered far too provincial to appear on restaurant menus, but one exception is the winter *arros amb fesol i naps* (rice with yellow swede/rutabaga and turnip). Another substantial dish is *el perrol*, a cauldron of rice stewed with meat and a large quantity of vegetables.

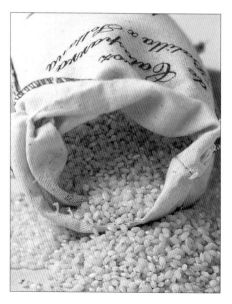

Paella

The birthplace of paella is the marshland outside the city of Valencia, round Lake Albufera. The area is still a place of ducks and eels. Bamboo groves standing in water separate lake from lake and little bridges carry small roads from village to village. El Palmar, one of the best-known villages, is surrounded by water.

Paella was invented here some 200 years ago. It is a summer dish, intended for picnics, and generally cooked by men in a flat pan set over a charcoal fire. Originally, paella used ingredients from the surrounding area – rice, garlic and parsley, either eels or snails, plus good beans, either flat green beans that look like runner beans or big flat kidney beans called *garrafones*. The seasoning was Spain's best – saffron – while the snails added a hint of rosemary. The rice is cooked very slowly, then covered with newspaper for the last 10 minutes, until all liquid has been absorbed. The paella is allowed to crisp slightly underneath before serving.

Saffron-yellow *paella valenciana*, decorated with mussels and strips of red (bell) pepper, prawns (shrimp) and chicken pieces like buried treasure, is eaten in Spain on every festive occasion. In Valencia, however, it is more of a tourist dish. Locals are more likely to opt for just shellfish or chicken; on the south coast, the usual choice is rabbit.

PASTA

Pasta has been eaten in Spain for longer than it has in north Italy. (There is even a recipe for a noodle soup in Catalonia's first printed cook book, by Rupert de Nolan, in 1477.) Pasta became everyday food in Spain and Italy at the same time, in the late 18th century. Durum wheat, used to make pasta, was planted in Catalonia in the 1950s. Today pasta is made in Andalusia and Extremadura.

The Catalan favourite is *fideos*, a thin, short spaghetti used in soups or served with sauces and sausage. South of paella country is Gandía (home of the

Above: Macaroni is a popular pasta, usually served with grated cheese.

Borgias, the family of Pope Alexander VI) where they have a *fideuá* (noodle) festival every year. The big pasta dish these days is shellfish with *fideos* instead of rice, which is a great deal easier to make than paella. It was invented in the 1970s and now features along the entire coast from Málaga to the Costa Brava, including one version where the pasta is dry-fried first.

Canelones (cannelloni) were introduced to Spain by the many Italian chefs who came to work in Barcelona in the 19th century. Flat dry squares, *obleas* (thin wafers), are now sold for making lasagne or for rolling into *canelones*. Home-made pasta was originally made by poor shepherds. They added simple flour-and-water paste squares (Manchego wafers) to stews such as *andrajos*.

Below: Fideos is a thin and short Spanish pasta – about 5cm/2in long.

Ten tips to good paella

Good paella is not difficult to make, but there are a few simple steps to ensure perfect results.

• Use a wide pan – 20cm/8in is right for two people. A deep pizza pan can be substituted for a paella pan.

• Use paella (or risotto) rice. Use 50–75g/2–3oz/generous ¼–scant ½ cup per person. (Don't stint on the rice.)

• Don't overdo the extras; they are there to flavour the rice. Choose a theme such as rabbit or shellfish.

• Don't be mean with the saffron, and use threads not powder. 0.1g is sufficient for two to three people and for six you will need 0.3g.

• Start with double the amount of stock to the volume of rice – some rices take more. Taste and warm the stock before adding it to the pan, making sure it is deeply flavoured. If the stock is insipid, so will be the paella.

• Don't overfill the pan; a depth of 2cm/¾in is about right.

• Use a wide heat source. Ideally the heat source should equal the diameter of the pan. The Spanish have special wide gas rings for making paella. Cooking over charcoal works well and solid fuel cookers are also suitable.

• If the heat source is smaller than the base of the pan, move the pan every 2–3 minutes, to prevent the middle cooking while the outside remains uncooked.

• The shape and size of the pan and the heat source are the main problems outside Spain. If in doubt, cover the pan with foil and bake in the oven for the second half of the cooking time.

• Let the paella stand, covered, off the heat for 10 minutes at the end of the cooking time, to absorb the last of the liquid. Paella should be a "dry" rice dish.

FRESH FISH

Spain is second only to Japan in fish consumption, with over 500g/1lb eaten per head per week. its capital, Madrid, though fr from the sea, has been called "the biggest port in Europe".

The two coasts of Spain are very different. From the wild Atlantic around Cape Finisterre, come the finest fish in the world. The Mediterranean, lazy and warm, is better for shellfish than fish, the best being caught outside Gibraltar.

Farming fish for salting goes back to Roman times, and today fish from salt flats such as Murcia's *Mar Menor* are prized for their extra flavour. The *salinas* off Cadiz raise gilthead bream, and sea bass and turbot are bred in El Grove on the Galician coast.

Cadiz is probably home to the original take-away (take-out) fried fish shop. Frying is something the Spanish do superbly well, although battered fried fish, called *a la romana*, is credited to the Italians. Málaga is famed for its mixed *pescaito frito*.

Spain shares the general Mediterranean love of fish stews and some say that the Spanish *bulla baissa* was the origin of French *bouillabaisse*. *Romesco de peix* (mixed fish with Catalan chilli), *zarzuela*, and the similar *suquet*, are incontestably Spanish. On the north coast, and in Galicia, the great *caldieras* layer mixed fish with potatoes. The east coast has *calderos* with rice, which include *cabracho* (the rascasse or large-scaled scorpion fish), the indispensable fish for soups and for making the broth of rice dishes.

Above (from front): Gilthead bream, red bream and blackhead bream

Below: Delicately flavoured hake is one of Spain's best-loved fish.

EVERYDAY FISH

The most popular everyday fish is salt cod (*bacalao*), then *pescadilla* – a small hake which is fried in a ring, with its tail in its mouth – and many small flat fish such as *gallo* (a type of plaice).

Sardines have an honoured place in Spanish cuisine, with festivals in Bilbao and elsewhere dedicated to the fish. They are enjoyed as an outdoor food and the *moraga*, on the Málaga coast, marks the beginning of summer: fish are skewered on to bamboo sticks, like sails on a tall mast, and are cooked beside the fires on the beaches. Mackerel, *caballo* and *melva* (from warm water) are other popular fish.

Left: Sardines are popular all over Spain and the freshly caught fish are often cooked on the beach, on the south and north coasts.

LUXURY FISH

Sea bass (*lubina*), turbot (*rodaballo*) and monkfish (*rape*, or *pixin* as it is known in Asturias) are cooked in wine and shellfish sauces, or with cider and potatoes. Really good fish needs no disguise and *ajada* (a simple mixture of oil, garlic and paprika) frequently partners fish in the north, in the same way that lemons do in the south. A typical dish is *besugo a la espalda*, in which red bream is spatchcocked on the grill and finished with garlic, hot chilli and a few drops of vinegar.

Dorada, the gilthead bream is the finest Mediterranean bream. Like the related *urta*, the sea bream lives on a diet of shellfish, which scents the flesh. Sea bream is most famously cooked with brandy and tomatoes.

Hake (*merluza*), with its delicate flavour and flaky texture, is extremely popular in Spain. It is often partnered with green sauces of asparagus or parsley. The back of the neck may be roasted, and *kokotas* (triangles cut from the lower throat) are a true speciality, often served in *pil pil* (a hot emulsion of garlic and oil). The *lenguado* (Dover or Channel sole) has a major fishing ground in the Bay of Biscay, while grey mullet (*mújol* or *lisa*) is popular in the Levante. Red mullet (*salmonetes*) are beloved by everyone in Spain.

Tiny *chanquetes* (whitebait) now have to be protected to retain stocks, but little anchovies (*boquerones*) are popular everywhere, though they are mainly fished in the Bay of Biscay. Anchovies are one of the best fish for frying and may be presented Málaga-style, fried in a fan pattern. More often they are marinated for tapas because they deteriorate so fast.

Elvers

Angulas, tiny baby eels, are a speciality of the *cofradías*, the Basque all-male gastronomic societies. Once considered only good enough to be fed to pigs, elvers are now an expensive delicacy, eaten around Christmas.

European eels spawn in the Sargasso Sea, between the West Indies and the Azores. The spawn set off for home and, amazingly, they head for the rivers from which their parents came, for example the Nervión, near Bilbao. The elvers of Aguinaga (west of San Sebastián) are the most highly prized. After a three-year journey back across the Atlantic, the elvers grow to 10cm/2in. They are washed ten times, then dipped in a cold tobacco solution to kill them. Sold cooked, they are then tossed in a hot earthenware bowl with oil and garlic. Once cooked, they look rather like spaghetti with only their eyes indicating that they are fish.

Elvers are also bred in Northern Ireland and France for sale in the Spanish market. These are softer and whiter than their wild cousins.

Above: Swordfish is a delicious, meaty fish that is very pink when raw but turns a greyish colour when cooked.

Above: Shark loin is good marinated with aromatic saffron and grilled.

TUNA, SWORDFISH AND SHARK

Tuna are landed at Vigo, from ships that trawl the world. They are also fished off Zahara de los Atunes (outside Gibraltar) with nets in the *alamadraba* – a bloody ritual that goes back as far as Roman times, where men fight the fish.

Tuna steaks are meaty and nutritious, and may be fried, grilled (broiled) or cooked on the barbecue. *Bonito del norte*, white tuna, is cooked in stews with (bell) peppers and potatoes. In Tarragona it is eaten *all cremat* (pot-roast with caramelized garlic).

Swordfish (*pez espada*) is ideal for grilling. Dogfish (*cazón*) and sharks such as *cailón* (porbeagle/mackerel shark) are good marinated and grilled.

FRESHWATER FISH

Spain has many fast-flowing rivers in its mountainous regions. Trout catches in some Pyrenees rivers run at 1,500 a day. León has about 3,000km/1,800 miles of trout rivers, as well as lakes. Brown trout abound in the rivers of western Asturias; *truchas del Bierzo* are well known. *Rea* (sea trout or salmon trout) run up the Galician *rías* (coastal inlets). Brown trout with *jamón serrano* is a famous combination, but otherwise cooking is simple, with fish being poached in cider or the Basque wine, *txacoli*.

Salmon teem in the rivers of Galicia and swim up into the Picos de Europa, south of Santander. Arriondas is the salmon capital of Spain. The same story is told here, as in Scotland, of labourers refusing to eat salmon more than three times a week. The classic salmon recipe is to salt them for one hour, then fry in pork fat. *Lamprea* (lamprey) follow the salmon, especially in the river Miño, while other fish, such as tench, carp and barbel are very much in evidence in Extremadura in summer.

Below: Brown and rainbow trout flourish in the rivers and lakes of Spain.

PRESERVED FISH

The Spanish adore preserved fish, and it is still weekly fare across the country. *Bacalao* is salt cod, which has been used in dishes for centuries. Other fish are salted too, including sardines and anchovies. Numerous fish and shellfish are canned – sometimes simply in brine, in rich, fruity olive oil, or in a spicy marinade such as *escabeche*. Fish caviars are a speciality.

BACALAO

It is ironic that the most commonly eaten fish in Spain – cod – is one that swims on neither of her shores. The Basques fished cod more than a millennium ago off the Gulf of St Lawrence, in the North Atlantic, and brought it back to Spain in salt. With the discovery of the Americas, the Basques were driven away by other fleets and a new fishing ground was established around Iceland and Norway.

Bacalao was called the inland fish, and was sold as stiff kite-shaped boards. With Catholic Spain imposing a Friday fast and a fast for the 40 days of

Below: Salt cod, known as bacalao, *is immensely popular and has remained weekly fare in Spain for centuries.*

Lent, it became a fixture in the Spanish diet. In these less religious days, where refrigeration is commonplace, *bacalao* has remained popular – probably due to the exquisite balance of salt and fish. In warmer climes, the flavour appears to deepen and salt tastes better in the south than it does in the colder north.

In Madrid, Bilbao and Barcelona, whole shops (*bacalao* boutiques) are devoted to the one product. The fish is sold like meat, ready cut and labelled with the place of origin and the dishes for which the cut is suitable. You can buy loin, strips and cheaper, thinner tail ends. The fatter, whiter Norwegian cuts are preferred for fillet dishes such as the Catalan *a la llauna*. Scottish *bacalao* is yellower and stronger tasting, and should be cooked with rice or potatoes. There are modern cures such as *bacalao inglés* that require less soaking.

There are over 100 classic *bacalao* dishes and many books devoted to *bacalao*. There is even a competition held at Guernika for the best new dish. *Bacalao* dishes are classed as red or white, according to whether they are made with, or without, tomatoes. *Bacalao al ajo arriero* contains tomato and red (bell) peppers. Best of the

white dishes is *bacalao pil-pil*. In this dish, the fish is cooked with garlic in oil in an earthenware dish (which retains heat) and is then swung for 15 or so minutes, until the gelatine in the fish skin combines with the oil to make a light, mayonnaise-like sauce.

Salt cod can be eaten at any time of the day. The fishermen in the north eat it for breakfast as *zurruputuna* (salt cod prepared with garlic, chillies and soaked bread). *Purrusaldo* is a robust soup made with salt cod, leek and potato. *Potaje de cuaresma*, made with salt cod, chickpeas and chard, is thought to have come from the monastery of Yuste and is eaten during Holy Week. The Cuenca area has a brandade-style dish, a purée of fish, potato and pine nuts. One of the best-known tapas dishes is *soldaditos de Pavia*, named after the Hussars in their yellow coats – sticks of salt cod are battered, then deep-fried until crisp and golden.

Raw salt cod salads are also very popular. *Rinrán* is a dish of salt cod with potato, olives and (bell) peppers. The Andalusian version of *remojón* pairs salt cod with sliced orange, and in Catalan *esqueixada* it is accompanied by red (bell) peppers and tomatoes.

Buying and soaking bacalao

The thinner cuts of salt cod are fin and tail pieces and are used to make puréed dishes such as salt cod fritters and soup. The fish doubles in weight during soaking, but half of this will be lost when the skin and bone are removed and discarded. The thickest pieces come from the loin and are used to make dishes such as *pil pil*.

Salt cod requires a minimum of 24 hours soaking, with 2–3 changes of water (more often in summer, because the soaking fish can smell pretty bad). The fish needs to retain some salt to maintain the interest of flavour and texture, but how long to soak the fish is a matter of personal judgement and depends on the dish being prepared.

In Andalusia the custom is to toast the fish first, break it up and then soak it. This has produced a range of dishes called *tiznao* that taste faintly of the fire.

CURED AND PRESERVED FISH

Mahogany-coloured *mojama* is the salted, wind-dried back flesh of the bluefin tuna (*atún*) and is a speciality of Seville and Cadiz. *Mojama* used to be street food, but it is becoming less common. It is similar to dried beef and, at its best, the thin ruby-coloured slices are almost transparent.

Canned tuna is Spain's second fish and is eaten weekly by most Spanish families. White albacore *atún blanco* (or *bonito del norte*), the long-finned tuna, is the world's best canned fish – and widely believed to be better canned than fresh. The most common of the tunas, *atún claro*, the yellow fin, is caught off the Cantabrian coast. It has darker and less dense meat – *ventresca* (belly) being the best.

Larger sardines are salted, both in the north and in Huelva in the south, where they are packed in large barrels. Sardine canning is also a major industry throughout Galicia.

Anchovies are also salted, and are called *anchoas* when canned in oil. In the north, some anchovies are brine-pickled before being packed in

Below: Fine Spanish anchoas are canned in olive oil.

Above: White albacore is the finest type of canned tuna.

Left: Canned sardines are widely eaten in Spain and are offered in many ways.

oil, and may also be smoked. Catalan La Escala, in the bay of Las Rosas, has a D.O. rating and here anchovies are salt-cured for a year – a process known as tanning – before being packed in oil in glass jars.

Some 140 varieties of fish and shellfish are canned in Galicia. The range of canned shellfish is enormous – from plump clams to scallops and mussels in spicy sauces such as *escabeche*. Tiny squid are canned in their ink, octopus in a variety of sauces, and there are also less familiar delights such as "crab thumbs" (the thickest part of the claw).

FISH CAVIARS

Luxurious caviars are a speciality of the Mediterranean. *Huevas de marucca*, from ling, are among the most common; the tiny salty eggs are sold in blocks cut from the pressed roe. The best caviar comes from the Murcian salt lagoons, from the grey mullet and is called *huevas de mújol de Mar Menor*. Before sturgeon caviar reached

Europe, this was used to make the great *botargo* (dark shavings cut from the pressed salted roe). Mixed and single moist roes packed into small jars are also sold and exported. These fish roes are particularly good served with eggs. Golden-brown *huevas de atún* come from the bluefin tuna, and have a sharp, faintly metallic taste. Other roes include the poorest cod (*capelán*), black herring roe and huge red salmon eggs, while restaurants offer caviars from sea bream, hake and anchovy.

Above: Black herring roe (back left) and grey mullet mújol, *or* shikrán, *(front left and right) are both good moist caviars.*

Below: Pressed huevas de marucca *(salted ling roe) is a delicacy but is widely available throughout the country.*

SHELLFISH

Atlantic currents, sweeping on to Cape Finisterre, bring food to an incredible range of shellfish on Europe's most westerly corner, to the Galician *rías* (coastal inlets) and the Spanish north coast. In these waters shellfish grow at great speed. In the Mediterranean the continental shelf is perfect for shellfish. The Spanish are really spoilt for choice.

Spanish shellfish are cooked to demonstrate their superb quality, usually either simply boiled or cooked *a la parrilla* (on the barbecue). Sea salt, and perhaps lemon wedges, are the common accompaniments.

SCALLOPS AND MUSSELS

Santiago de Compostela in Galicia is famous for scallops, and the pilgrims have chosen their shell for their badge. Today scallops are farmed in the quiet bays to the west. Large ones, *vieras*, and little *zamburiñas* (queens or bay scallops) are cooked with their orange roe curled round them. Scallops may be breadcrumbed and fried, cooked with wine and chilli, or with tomato sauce (in St James' style). They feature in the flat Galician pie that is prepared for special occasions.

The mussel beds of Galicia are famous, and Tarragona in the east is also an important mussel area. The bivalves are grown on ropes secured

to platforms, out in the western bays. In Galicia, 2.5 million mussels are canned per day, and there are plenty of fresh ones for the whole of Spain, too. It is their sheer size and tenderness that astounds. They are large enough to be breadcrumbed and fried, although wine and parsley mixtures, sometimes with bacon, are more usual. They are also added to many fish dishes and stews. A favourite tapas dish in Madrid is *tigres* – mussels in béchamel sauce with a little chopped (bell) pepper, breadcrumbed then grilled.

CLAMS AND COCKLES

In Spain clams are common fare. They are boiled for tapas, added to soups and pasta, and used to garnish grander dishes. They are fished on both coasts, but the northern ones are plumper, and a regional speciality. There are many varieties; one of the best is the *almeja fina* (the carpetshell). Most magnificent is the *concha fina* (Venus), which measures about 8cm/3in across, with orange flesh inside. It is opened to order in the sherry bars of the south.

Other bivalves include common cockles, the dog cockle, *almendra de mar*, razor shells and *ostíon*, the Portuguese oyster, found on the Cantabrian coast.

Percebes

One of the world's most expensive shellfish, *percebes* are known in English as goose barnacles. You understand why if you see them crowded on the storm-washed rocks. Fixed at the foot, reaching perhaps 5cm/2in high, blackish or mottled, they look like a gaggle of geese with outstretched necks, particularly so because the tips are pointed and white, like a beak.

Percebes are either left raw or briefly boiled. Their orange flesh is squeezed from its casing and served with vinaigrette. Their taste is "essence of seawater".

Left: Carpetshell clams are very popular and are most often served in sauces.

PRAWNS AND SHRIMPS

Saltwater varieties are fished on both coasts. In size order:

Camarones These are the tiniest Spanish shrimps and are caught around Cadiz. They turn white, rather than pink, when cooked, and are made into delicious little fritters.

Quisquilla This term covers all the smaller varieties of prawn (shrimp) that are caught in their thousands off the Spanish coasts. They are added to scrambled eggs and stuffings, or used to add interest to *ensaladilla* (diced vegetable salad) and various sauces.

Gamba These have a good colour and are fished reasonably deep, giving them a good flavour. They are used in some of Spain's most famous dishes. *Gambas en gabardinas* (in overcoats) are battered then fried, while the southern dish *gambas pil pil* (which is quite different from northern *pil pil*) is based on chilli, and is very hot.

Langostino These are the longest Mediterranean prawn, fished from deep water. Sometimes they are called tiger prawns, as some varieties are striped. They are served simply to show off their true flavour – for example in salads.

Below: Cigalas (scampi) have a fabulous flavour and are fished on every coast.

Carabinero These prawns grow to 20cm/8in long and are a deep scarlet colour with a violet head. (They are named after the red coats worn by the military.) They lack the flavour of *langostinos* but are excellent in northern matured bean dishes, where the prawn heads add flavour, and in display salads, because the bodies retain their delightful red markings after shelling.

LOBSTERS

Bogavante, the true lobster, is party fare, while *langosta* (in Castilian), the spiny lobster (saltwater crayfish) is eaten to celebrate Spain's national day. Squat (or slipper) lobsters, called *cigarra* in Spain, make cricket-like noises under water. They have insignificant claws, but stocky little tails. St James even has his own lobster, the *santiaguiño*, with a cross on its head.

Scampi (*cigala* or *escarmarlan grande* in Catalan) are "false lobsters". They are a luxury, and four or five make a good portion. Their splendid heads have beady eyes, their long straight claws are pink and scarlet even when raw. They go very well with mayonnaise.

Right: Gambas are probably the best of all prawns and have a wonderful flavour and lovely texture.

Freshwater crustaceans

Crayfish (*cangrejos*) are found in the Duero and Tago rivers. There are festivals to celebrate them in Herrera del Pisuergo and at Palencia where the locals eat them in great numbers.

Tiny crayfish also flourish in freshwater reservoirs all over Spain. These crustaceans are sold as *embalsadores* (behind the dam) and are used to make a range of good sauces and soups.

Right: The spider crab is known as centollo *or* txangurro *in Spain.*

CRABS

Small shore crabs, such as *necoras*, which have red knees, are served simply boiled, and picked to pieces at the table. They make ideal beach food. *Buey de mar* (ox of the sea) is the large-clawed crab, but the favourite, particularly on the north coast, is the spider crab (*centollo* in Castilian), great beasts on akimbo legs, with stronger and sweeter meat. The classic Basque dish is *txangurro* (dressed meat in the shell); there is one crab per person.

SQUID, CUTTLEFISH AND OCTOPUS

Common to both oceans, squid are universal and a popular food. Few travellers have visited a Spanish beach and not eaten *calamares* (fried squid rings in batter). There are many varieties of squid, and they can vary considerably in size. Their pink skin turns grey after a time on shore, so choose fresh pink ones when buying. They are also commonly sold cut into rings for stews and should be cooked fast or very slowly, otherwise they will become rubbery. On the north coast, where they are known as *raba*, breaded squid are popular.

Cuttlefish, called *jibia* or *sepia*, and *chocos* and *chiperones* if tiny, are very similar to squid but rounder in shape. They are often sold without the skin when their colour is milky white. When cleaning, be very careful to remove the ink sacs intact because the ink stains. Slit the body open to remove the broad white cuttle bone.

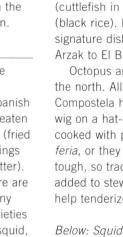

The flesh of the cuttlefish is thick and sweeter than squid. It is ideal for slow simmering or cooking stuffed. The black ink is also used in cooking and classic dishes include *sepia en su tinto* (cuttlefish in their ink) and *arroz negro* (black rice). Ink also features in many signature dishes in top restaurants from Arzak to El Bullí.

Octopus are particularly popular in the north. All the bars in Santiago de Compostela have one sitting like a great wig on a hat-stand. They are mainly cooked with paprika, as in *pulpo de feria*, or they are stewed. Octopus are tough, so traditionally wine corks are added to stews, which are thought to help tenderize the flesh.

Below: Squid are popularly fried in rings, grilled or stuffed and braised.

BEEF, VEAL, LAMB AND KID

The varieties of meat (*carne*) available in Spain are far wider than elsewhere. The middle classes eat a great deal of meat, while the working classes eat comparatively little; there is virtually no vegetarian cooking. Pulse and vegetable dishes are invariably flavoured with sausages and pork fat.

BEEF AND VEAL

The Spanish have never been great beef eaters. Richard Ford, a century ago, remarked that "bulls are bred for baiting and oxen for the plough, not the spit".

High temperatures elsewhere mean the best beef comes from the north, and Galicia produces about two-thirds of Spanish beef. However, new breeding programmes, and the modern practice of moving cattle indoors, means more beef is now being produced in Catalonia, Aragón and the cereal plains of Castile. Only the Basques will eat "bloody" meat, and red meat is exported in return for veal cattle. The native breed is mahogany-red *retinto*. *Morucho* and *avilana* are work animals.

Spain has at least three sorts of beef. Hung beef is a northern taste, and vast *chuletones* (chops) are enjoyed in this region. Cattle are slaughtered at between two and five years old to produce *carne de buey* (ox) or *vaca* (cow). This lesser quality beef is stewed, famously with chocolate, or with vegetables as in the Catalan *estofat*. Meatballs are sold in every bar and are loved by children, too. Cuts such as salt brisket go into stews.

Younger beef is the popular choice; *añojo* means yearling although, in fact, the cattle are slaughtered at between 10 and 18 months. Joints of meat are frequently labelled with their age and diet. For example, *lomo cebón* is loin fattened on barley.

Above: Ox tail, or bull's tail, benefits from long, slow cooking and is a very popular choice when stewed.

Ternera translates as veal, but it is pink or grey veal, not white. Veal calves are never intensively reared in Spain, and they are often four times the age of Dutch or Italian calves when they are slaughtered. Only in Ávila are calves killed very young. One veal of note is the northern *ternera gallega*, D.O., which comes from the honey-blond *rubio* cattle.

Veal escalopes (US scallops) may be braised with vegetables or fried. *Filetitos* are small escalopes fried with lemon juice, and six or seven make up a single portion. Veal is wonderful with artichokes and sherry, or in stews with young vegetables.

Above: Brisket is a popular addition to stews such as cocido. *Cuts from ox or cow are used to make casseroles.*

Below: Veal fillet is usually cut into escalopes. One universal dish is San Jacobo, *in which the fillet is topped with* serrano *ham, then cheese.*

The Moorish oven
Domed ovens built of *adobe* (roofing bricks), which hold the heat, rather than firebricks, are prized for roasting tiny lambs and piglets particularly in Castile, in places such as Aranda de Duero and Haro. These ovens are part of the restaurant structure, and are about 2m/6ft in diameter inside. They are wood-fired, and cooking only takes place when the glowing charcoal subsides. The burned-out coals are pushed to the side, the dishes are put into the oven using long paddles, then the door is sealed. In the hot south, similar ovens are built outside houses for domestic use.

THE FIGHTING BULL

The fighting bull is either slaughtered at the age of one, and the meat is minced (ground), or it lives a life of luxury until it comes to the ring at the age of three or four. The meat from these bulls (*toro de lidia*) is sold in specialist shops. Ex-matadors frequently buy restaurants, and a number of these source beef from the local bullring. The meat is deep black-red (though not tough) and is eaten as steaks in sherry in Jerez, or minced or stewed. The *rabo* (tail) is a popular choice for hotpots, while the testicles – the matadors' titbit – may be breadcrumbed and fried. Valencia produces a special bull ham.

LAMB AND KID

Lamb is very expensive, but it is still the traditional meat in the grazing regions of central and western Spain, and up into the mountains of Aragón and Murcia. Elsewhere, it is an Easter or wedding treat. Spain has 24 million sheep – the same number as when Napoleon marched there during the Peninsular War (1808–14) – which dominate the Meseta, the high heart of Spain. They spend the winter in Extremadura and southern Castile, and once walked north in vast flocks (the *transhumance*) to summer pastures in Cantabria. However, today sheep are transported by train, with Burgos as the commercial sheep centre.

Thyme is used to flavour roast lamb. Lamb chops are popular, and tiny legs of lamb provide an exquisite eating experience. Stews can consist of a whole animal, chopped. *Cochifrito* is flavoured with lemon or vinegar and paprika; *chilindrones*, around Logroño traditionally feature a mild red chilli pepper. *Menestra* are spring stews cooked with young vegetables.

Mutton is used in a few dishes in Aragón and Extremadura, and some of the classic stews such as *chilindrón* and *caldereta* originally used mutton.

Kid (*cabrito* or *choto*) is another luxury meat, either cooked on a spit or in traditional stews such as *tumbet* in Valencia or *caldereta extremeña*, which is thickened with the kid's puréed liver.

Spanish stews

Olla puchero Both these words mean cooking pot, the large vessel used to make the daily stew cooked by many families in Spain.

Olla podrida Literally meaning rotten pot, the name of this stew actually means hotchpotch – a mixed stew of beef, bacon, ham and vegetables, simmered so long the ingredients become very soft-textured.

Cocido Meaning boiled or simmered, *cocido* is shorthand for mixed stew.

Cocido madrileño This is the national dish, where several different meats are cooked with chickpeas and fresh vegetables. It makes a three-course feast. Made all over the country, the meat content is reduced the further from the capital you get; every region includes its own sausages and other produce. The Basques like to add red beans, and in Seville both rice and chickpeas are included, with garlic, sweet potatoes and *morcilla* sausage. In the south pears and pumpkins are often used, and in the Canaries, sweet potatoes and fresh corn are added.

Escudella This is the Catalan word for *cocido* or stew. *Escudella i carn d'olla* is a big dish, with the *carn* (pork) as one large dumpling, or it may contain a selection of ham, chicken, veal and *botifarra* sausage, with chickpeas and noodles, plus vegetables. The liquid is served first as soup, the rest follows. *Escudella de pagès* is a country-style stew, with carrots, potatoes and cabbage.

Fabada This is the Asturian stew of dried beans, salt pork and ham, with oak-smoked *morcilla* and *chorizo*.

Caldereta Meaning witch's cauldron, this is the name of the lamb, goat or fish stew that is cooked in it.

Estofado *Estofat* in Catalan, this is meat that is slow-cooked, usually in its fat and juice.

Guiso Also known as *guisado*, this is simply a stew with sauce.

Cochifrito Pieces of lamb or goat are fried, and seasoned with vinegar or lemon and paprika.

Fricandó Small veal pieces are stewed with vegetables such as carrots. The Catalan version contains onions and tomatoes.

Above: In Spain, legs of lamb may be very small – with one leg per person.

Above: Kid is a luxury meat that often replaces lamb in traditional stews.

PORK

The pig represents Spain's history and religion on the plate. To eat pork and sausages became, after the unification of the country at the end of the fifteenth century, a way of demonstrating nationality. (The Muslim Moors and the Jews were forbidden to eat pork.) In a poor, mountainous country, the pig provided the major source of nutrition, and it is still Spain's most widely eaten meat.

Almost every family would once have owned a pig. People in the villages would throw their rubbish into local gullies and streams, and this waste sustained foraging pigs. People who live in apartments in Madrid will still tell you about the family porker in Galicia. The *matanza* (pig killing), when families gather to make sausages and celebrate, is the greatest non-religious festival of the year.

Although cured meat is eaten more often than fresh, pork chops and loin of pork remain Spain's most familiar meat. *Solomillo*, which means fillet of beef in the north, becomes pork in the south; it is delicious *a la trianera* (roasted with sherry). *Magro* is a pork steak, commonly served with a tomato sauce or potatoes. *El frite*, or *cochefrito*, is chopped fried meat flavoured with

Above: Loin chops are popular in beach bars.

Above: Chump chops are great cooked on la plancha, *the iron grill sheet.*

vinegar and paprika; it is traditionally prepared to test the meat of a newly killed pig. Minced (ground) pork is used in dishes such as *pringa* and *prueba*, which were both devised as a way to test the spicing mix, before stuffing the meat into sausage casings. *Gazpacho manchego* is a delicious coarse pork pâté, and is quite different from the well-known southern gazpacho.

Other cuts of pork are cured, as well as the ubiquitous ham. In the north, the famous cured meat is *lacón*, a front-leg ham. Among the *salazones* (salted meats), there is coarse-salted belly, and also *panceta* (streaky bacon), which is sometimes marinated before being cured and/or smoked. *Torreznos* are pork slices, fried like bacon and served with eggs, a popular dish in the centre of the country and Extremadura. However, their social status is indicated by their name in Cervantes novel, *Don Quixote, duelos y quebrantes*, which means sorrow and suffering.

Below: In Spain, pork loin is trimmed to the meat eye only.

THE BLACK WILD PIG

The native *ibérico* pig is known by its black trotter (*pata negra*). (The phrase *pata negra* is also a slang term used to describe anything good.) There are actually four dark-skinned breeds, the main two having black or red hair. The pigs are trim and graceful, with long legs. They run wild in small groups, in the *sierras* of Andalusia and particularly in Extremadura, in the flower pastures under the holm oaks, called the *dehesa*.

Their numbers are decreasing as their fame rises. Their final food is acorns, which give the meat its full flavour and an old golden tinge. If meat is labelled *bellota*, it means the pig fed entirely on acorns and will therefore have excellent flavour.

Wild pigs are slaughtered at 18 months, weighing about 160kg/ 352lb – the domestic hog reaches that weight at nine months. Highly prized for ham, they now make up only five per cent of Spanish *serrano* (compared with 25 per cent in the 1950s), 90 per cent of which is taken up by restaurants. Another restaurant speciality is fresh steaks of *cerdo ibérico*; it is dark like beef and tastes like game.

Below: Spanish panceta *is fresh or cured belly. If it is unavailable, Italian pancetta makes an excellent substitute.*

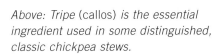

Above: Tripe (callos) *is the essential ingredient used in some distinguished, classic chickpea stews.*

Cooking with pork fat

Pork fat (*manteca*) adds a very characteristic flavour to many Spanish dishes. *Manteca colorada* is fat coloured with paprika. It is delicious spread on bread for breakfast in the south. The fat is also made into *rillettes* (fat packed around cooked, shredded pork).

Tocino is solid fat, fresh or salted, back or belly, for cubing and frying. Like *panceta* (fresh or cured pork belly), it adds flavour and goodness to pulse dishes. Dry or poor-quality *serrano* ham is chopped and used for cooking.

SUCKLING PIG

Truly a wonder, so small and so tender, the suckling pig is known as *cochinillo* in Castilian, *tostón* in central Spain and *porcella* in the Balearics.

Old Castile is famous for its ovens, which are used to roast either milk-fed piglets or lamb. The west, Arévolo and Segovia, is piglet country. There they are roasted in a huge domed brick or refractory oven, heated by holm oak – just imagine thirty piglets sizzling on a revolving turntable.

With the pig being killed at 15 to 20 days old, the shoulder blade is only the size of a car key. To roast the pigs, they are split through the belly and opened out flat with their legs and tail out. Each splayed pig is displayed in an earthenware dish, which catches the fat and juices as the pig roasts. The roasted meat is carved using the side of a plate.

Above right: Calf's liver is good cooked with sweet Málaga wine sauce.

Right: Strongly flavoured pig's liver is stewed on the first day of pig killing with sweet, pungent sauces.

OFFAL

It is said that everything from the pig can be eaten except its squeak. The pig is the principal source of offal (variety meats) in Spain, although other animals are also used.

Pigs' heads and tails can be salted. Pickled ears are breaded and fried, as well as being used to make some wonderful delicatessen salads. Trotters and tails may be found in stews and rice dishes. Ham bones are used to flavour beans; as they grow older they become highly prized, with neighbours lending each other bones for stews. Pig's caul is used to baste faggots, and ham fat (*unto*) sold in great rolls, is used for frying – aged fat is prized in Galicia for its extra flavour.

Lamb and veal kidneys are to be found cooked in wine sauces in tapas bars. Sweetbreads (*mollejas*) are usually fried. Brains are used in two good gypsy dishes: they are minced (ground) to stuff *tortilla Sacromonte*; and are served fried, with lemon, as *sesos a la flamenca*. *Criadillas* (testicles) are called white kidneys; a delicacy for matadors, they are breadcrumbed and fried. Another "man's dish" is blood, solidified in squares with vinegar, which is offered in tapas bars.

The first dish to be eaten at the *matanza* (pig killing) is *asadura*, the liver and guts made into a great stew with almonds, garlic and oregano. The similar *chanfaina*, with lungs (lights) and liver, is cooked, often in vast vats for festivals. A more elegant calf's liver dish from the south contains sweet Málaga wine and aromatic herbs.

Tripe, called *menudo* in Andalusia, is one of the surprises of Spanish cuisine. Resembling a woollen blanket when raw, it has a repertoire of dishes. *Callos a la madrilena* (from veal or pig) is tavern fare in the capital city. It is seasoned with onion, thyme and tomato, and includes *morcilla*, chorizo and ham too. Depending on the region, tripe is usually cooked with chickpeas or beans, along with a ham bone for extra flavour. One Catalan dish combines tripe with potatoes, pine nuts and a glass of old *rancio* wine.

Pork tongues (*lengua*) are commoner than lambs' tongues. The former are cooked in a Majorcan dish, with pomegranate seeds. But larger veal tongues are also served cold, and as a *fiambre* (pressed delicatessen meat).

White *manitas*, lambs' feet, come 16 to a portion and leave pearl-like bones on the plate. *Zarajos* are the lamb's intestines; they are wrapped around two twigs, then grilled (broiled). Lambs' tails are eaten in Aragón, where they are called mountain asparagus, with (bell) peppers and tomatoes. In the markets you will find beef muzzles, too, and cow's heel with the horn off.

SAUSAGES

The pig is virtually a "larder on trotters" and is valued more for what can be made out of it than for fresh meat. It is turned into sausages, frequently home-made, which will last the whole year. The raw pork is minced (ground), or hand-chopped, mixed with back fat and spices, then stuffed into casings. The bigger the pieces of meat, and the lower the fat content, the sweeter the meat is.

Some sausages (chiefly *morcillas*) include extra ingredients such as onion or rice, and additions such as nuts are included in regions where there was once a strong Moorish presence. Garlic is used in the south and west, but too much would turn the sausage rancid. There are also sausages made using pork blends – with beef, vegetables other than onion, and even the occasional cereal sausage such as the *farinata* of Salamanca. There are game sausages too, made from venison.

The mixture is stuffed into casings made from pigs' guts. These natural casings vary in size so some sausages are fatter than others. The sausages are then hung on strings in the cold dry air and will lose as much as 35 per cent of their weight if left for a full year. Smoked sausages are found across Spain, usually coinciding with the old pilgrim routes, as in Bierzo in León. The dry sausages used in the Asturian *fabada* (pork and bean stew) are smoked and swell with cooking.

Sausages tend to be classed by colour, and this provides some guidance as to how they should be cooked and served. Many dried sausages may be eaten raw, although this is not always the rule.

BLACK SAUSAGES

Morcillas are blood puddings, and are the first to be made from the newly killed pig, straight after slaughter. They are made as links, or as rings in Seville and Ronda in the south. Once made, they are boiled in cauldrons, then dried for storage. Occasionally they may also be smoked, and they are almost always cooked again before being eaten.

These wonderful sausages are a speciality of the north, the most famous being those of Extremadura and Asturias, which are flavoured with aniseed and cloves, and plumped with either rice or onions. Rice is typically used in some parts of Aragón, and the Burgos *morcilla* also contains pine nuts. *Morcilla dulce* is eaten raw, and can be found in tapas bars. The spicing, sweetness and rich tongue-clinging fat make it irresistible.

Botifarra is the black sausage from the east of the country. It is made in links, or occasionally in rings. The *bisbe* (meaning

Left: Ring-shaped black and white botifarras *are made in Catalonia.*

Above: The fat chorizo from Cantimpalo, and the ring-shaped one from Jabugo are two famous versions of this classic spicy paprika sausage.

bishop) is an outsize sausage, while the *bull* contains tongue and cheek. There are Valencian *morcillas* too, which are sometimes very spicy, and a Majorcan version, *camiot*, which is flavoured with cumin and cinnamon.

RED SAUSAGES

Paprika is used in sausages right across Spain, apart from in Catalonia, the Levante and the Balearics (except for the *sobrasada* from Majorca). Chorizos are named after the *choricero* chilli that gives them both spiciness and colour. There are at least 50 varieties of chorizo, but two main types.

Red chorizos, made in links, contain minced (ground) meat, which is mottled with fat. They may be fried or boiled. The longer varieties are usually sweeter, while small round ones are *picante* (hot and spicy). The knobbly, garlicky *chorizos de Cantimpalos*, from Segovia, are typical of central Spain and are the first choice for the Madrid *cocido* (the national stew of salt and fresh meats).

Above: Lomo *is not actually a sausage, but cured pork loin flavoured with herbs and spices.*

The second type is the tapas or cured chorizo. The meat filling is stuffed into a larger gut casing and so is much longer and fatter. These are sliced thinly and eaten with bread, or they are cut into little batons and added to salads. The meat in these sausages may be marbled or chopped.

There are many varieties of cured chorizo, and each one attracts an enthusiastic and loyal following. *Pamplona* resembles salami, with its thoroughly minced (ground) meat, and the coloured fat that looks like orange rice grains. *Chorizo de Rioja* has big swirls of paprika-red marbled meat around the fat. *Chistorra* is typically Basque and Navarran. This narrow, cigar-shaped sausage includes beef as well as pork. *Morcón* is widely distributed in Andalusia. It is made from marinated loin and shoulder, and seasoned with paprika. It is tied with string to make a round sausage that resembles a hand grenade. There is also a larger Murcian version. However, it is *sobrasada de Mallorca* that probably wears the crown and is the pride of the Balearic islands. The sausage is more or less spherical in shape, although it is sometimes long, and is air-cured for up to a year. It is spreadable and has a smooth pâté-like texture that is achieved by grinding and regrinding the pork several times. The sausage meat is also sold in pots.

Lomo embuchado (or *cinta*) looks like a sausage but is actually the spinal loin muscle (*caña*). It is marinated in garlic and paprika, sometimes with sugar, oregano and nutmeg, then encased and dried for two to six months. A good variety is produced in Teruel. It has a delicate flavour and compact texture, but is expensive so is quite a treat.

Sausages that are named after a place famed for ham also attract a following. *Jabugocitos* are little frying sausages from Jabugo, *guijuelo* is a fat tapas sausage from Extremadura, and *ibéricos* are made from the meat of the prized black pig.

Below: Long, fat cured salchichones *are sliced and served for tapas.*

WHITE SAUSAGES

Sausages that are neither black nor red are classified as white sausage, although they are not necessarily white in appearance. The cured varieties are a dark cerise colour inside and are cased in the smaller gut.

Salchichón comes in rings and strings, and is usually powdered on the outside with ambient bacteria. The meat and fat are easily distinguishable. Some famous examples are made in Vic in Catalonia. These sausages are dry, like salami, and laced with peppercorns. *Fuet* is a Catalonian sausage containing white pepper and sugar. It is long and thin so dries fast, and is consequently very chewy.

Longaniza covers a variety of sausages. A few are dry, while others are fresh and coiled in a bowl, and still more hang in a wonderful hank. Short lengths are used for cooking. If the sausages are thin, they tend to be hard, bland and can be rather fatty.

White *botifarras* (known as *blancas*) are the brothers of the black ones. These fresh sausages are usually grilled (broiled), and are often eaten with beans all along the east coast. And of course there are *embutidos* (fresh sausages) that are made everywhere.

Above: Fuet *is a chewy, dry Catalonian sausage.*

HAMS

Spain produces some of Europe's finest hams, one-third of which are exported. About one-fifth of Spanish pigs are used for hams, so it is not surprising more ham is eaten in Spain than elsewhere in Europe – the Basques alone eat nearly one whole ham each per year.

The mountain-cured *jamón serrano* rules supreme, but lesser hams – *jamón cocido* – are cured for boiling. The front leg of the pig (*paleta*, or *lacón* in Galicia) is also cured. It is a coarser cut but with a very even flavour). In the north-west it is used for *caldo gallego*, while *lacón con grelos* (with turnip tops) is definitely their national dish.

JAMON SERRANO

Serrano is the adjective from *sierra* (mountain). It means mountain ham, and indicates that it is raw and dried in cold air. Typically, these hams are long and thin, and almost triangular at the meaty end. Better ones are marketed with the trotter (foot) still attached.

Big names in ham production in Andalusia are Jabugo in the Aracena (near Huelva) and Trévelez, in the high mountains south of Granada. *Jabugo* is probably the Spanish choice for the best ham, but *Trévelez* is better known abroad. Being so far south, these hams need heavier salting, and so are less sweet and melt-in-the-mouth than hams from cooler climes such as those from Extremadura and Lérida.

Teruel in Aragón and *Guijuelo* in Salamanca have D.O. status for local hams. The former is famous for its white hams; the latter for lighter salting and sweet-flavoured hams. The whole

Below: Serrano *ham from the black* ibérico *pig is highly prized.*

of Extramadura is pig country and *Montanchez* in Cáceres and *Cumbre Mayores* are both popular hams.

As well as the big names, who don't need to advertise, as they sell all the ham that they can produce, there are also many small producers. Many hams are sold packed off the bone, or sliced. Other parts of the pig (including the loin and front shoulder) are also cured.

Thinly sliced *serrano* is eaten for tapas or sandwiched with cheese, but it is also used to wrap fish. Little batons are added to salads and bean dishes.

Breeds and grades

White hams come from crosses of Landrace, Duroc and the Large White pigs. Just 5 per cent of hams now come from the incomparable black native pig called *ibérico*. This ham is sold under this name *ibérico* abroad but, in Spain, it is known as *pata negra*. *Ibérico* meat is leaner and tougher than other pigs', while the surface fat attracts a little blue penicillin mould, which adds flavour.

These expensive "black" hams are graded by the animals' food. *Bellota* (acorn) indicates a pig fed in the wild, and this is terribly expensive. *Recebo* refers to a pig fed on a diet of grain and acorns for its last month. *Pienso* means the pig was entirely grain fed.

Above: Raw serrano *ham is cured in the cool air of the sierras.*

Curing

It takes 12 months to cure a *serrano* ham. All hams take at least 9 months to cure, and *pata negra* is cured for 18 months. The ham is salted once, for 40 to 60 days, then matured hanging in the dry winter air. When summer temperatures return, it is cellar-rested.

Fat

The fat is distributed between the muscles in fine layers, increasing the flavour of the meat. When black pigs forage on grass and acorns, this fat has a very high oleic oil content, and so liquifies at a lower temperature than other meat fats. It also has a lower cholesterol content than farmed or other free-range (farm-fresh) meat.

Carving

Serrano hams need their own stands to support them, as they are very long. They are carved into paper-thin slices, lengthways with the grain of the meat. The meat is faintly chewy, varying in colour from deep red to scarlet. The fat appears as tiny lengthways threads in the meat. The best cuts come from close to the bone on the *manza* (the rounder side).

Other salazones

Parts of lamb, kid and beef can also be salted, and smoked for more flavour. *Cecina* (*ceniza* in Catalan) is cured beef that is thinly sliced. There are also bull hams and duck breast hams.

THE BARNYARD

Poultry cluck around the many farms of Spain. However, the chickens are mainly kept for their eggs; the birds are not the main family meat.

CHICKEN

More popular now than it used to be, there was a time when chicken was more expensive than beef. The well-known Catalan dish, chicken with lobster, recalls its luxury status.

There are numerous Spanish chicken dishes, reflecting regional tastes and using local produce. Chicken is cooked with sherry in the south; with (bell) peppers in Rioja; *alli-pebre* (with garlic and paprika) in Valencia, and with tomatoes and cumin in Extremadura.

Below: The boiling hen is tastier than a young chicken and has its own repertoire of dishes in Spain.

Below: Huge capons are a favourite at Christmas time.

The smell of chickens roasting, basted with pork fat, in chicken shops at the weekend is quite mouthwatering.

Gallina is a boiling hen. In *gallina en pepitoria*, it is simmered slowly, then the sauce is thickened with ground nuts. Capons are sold in the Christmas market in Villalba in Galicia. These large birds weigh about 5kg/11lb. Some are fattened on maize (like foie gras ducks) and they are sold in Madrid dressed and stuffed with Roquefort or chestnuts.

Chicken offal (variety meats) is widely used. The gizzards are added to lentil dishes, and accompany the chicken meats in *arroces* (rice dishes). Chicken livers cooked in sherry is a popular tapas dish.

Above: Guinea fowl are regarded as a substitute for true game birds.

OTHER POULTRY

Goose and duck are cooked in Catalonia, but are not popular in the rest of Spain. Goose with pears (*oca amb peras*) is the famous dish of the region. The Catalans are known for combining birds and fruit, and the reason is not hard to discover – the birds feed on fruit. Duck is combined with figs in another Catalan classic.

Ducks (*pato*) are also reared in Valencia near lake Albufera but they are not widespread elsewhere. Catalonia and Navarra now breed the mallard (a cross between the white duck and the grey barbary), called *anèc* in Catalan. Because of the French influence in these regions, duck hams, foie gras and even duck confit are produced. In Galicia, a popular dish combines duck with turnips. However, Spain's most famous duck recipe comes from Seville. The juice of the Seville orange was added to duck to cut through the fat. Olives do the same job, and there are several dishes that combine duck and olives.

The turkey was introduced to Europe via Spain in the 16th century from America. Called *pavo*, after the peacock (*pavo real*), it was at first cooked like a peacock, stuffed and inserted into a pig's caul. The dark bronze or black turkey are the birds of choice, weighing in at around 3kg/6½–7lb. The best birds come from Aspe, in the Pyrenees.

The guinea fowl (*pintada*) came from Queen Dido's Africa – either directly, or with the Romans. They are now reared in Spain, as are quails (*codornices*).

GAME

Spain is great for wildlife, and out in the country the sign *coto de caza* (shooting reserved) is a constant reminder that hunting is a passion in Spain. *Caza mayor* (game hunting) has always been part of the social/political scene. *Caza menor* (shooting birds) can be pursued by anyone with a gun and a knapsack.

FEATHERED GAME

There are massive migrations of birds across Spain twice a year, on their way to and from Africa. The 27,000 Spanish shooting clubs try to ensure that two-thirds of the birds pass through their land, for breeding. Small birds have always contributed to the poor family's diet: fieldfare, starling, even sparrow, can be added to rice dishes.

Duck

In Spain, duck shooting (*aquatica*) is a specialized sport, with many adherents. There are mallards on all the lakes and salt flats in Spain, and many teal.

Below: The abundant pigeon is meaty and benefits from long, slow cooking.

Above: Tiny quail are one of the most prevalent wild birds found in Spain.

Pigeon

Present all year, pigeons (*palomas*) are netted as they fly over the mountains. They are pot-roasted with vinegar, or with raisins in the Val d'Arran, and stewed with peas or mushrooms in Castile. Murcia has a famous pigeon pie, which mimics the highly spiced Moroccan *b'stilla* (a pie made with filo pastry and a filling of shredded pigeon, ground almonds and spices), revealing its distinct Moorish influences. The pie is then baked until golden and sprinkled with icing (confectioners') sugar and ground cinnamon.

Partridge

The partridge in Spain is the red-legged (French) *perdiz* (which is larger than the grey-legged variety). It is far and away the most popular of game birds. It gorges on the sherry grapes in the south, and from October a million of the birds are eaten each year. La Mancha is the partridge capital of Europe. Once captured, the birds may be

Left: Teal is one of the smallest wild ducks and is highly prized for its fabulous taste and texture.

kept in cages until needed. Celebrated recipes include partridges in chocolate, Pyrenean mushroom stews, and *perdices en escabeche* (a salad of jellied, vinegared birds). They are also stewed with cabbage, in a dish that dates back to the 1400s, and with beans.

Quail

In Spain, it is said to rain quails, rather than cats and dogs because there are so many of these tiny birds (about 10 million), which are trapped in their thousands as they fly south each April. The birds are roasted, barded with bacon and stuffed with their own innards, or casseroled with wine and garlic, or with grapes. A speciality is *codornices con pochas*, quail with freshly shelled haricot (navy) beans, as their seasons coincide.

Woodcock

Chocha (woodcock) are found in Galicia in the winter. The small birds are shot for the pot, and you really need to allow two birds per person.

Pheasant

Because it was recorded by the great French chef, Escoffier, *faisan al modo de Alcántara*, pheasant stuffed with duck liver and truffles, became the most famous bird dish in Europe.

FURRED GAME

Ninety per cent of Spain is mountainous and full of game. The mountain goats are the long-horned ibex (*cabra monte*) and the short-horned chamois (*rebeco* in Catalan). Boars (*jabalí*) are hunted by moonlight. They are numerous in the rugged north and in the southern mountains. Because the wild boar does so much damage to young woodland, it is now culled. Boar is stewed with thyme or wine and nuts.

Venison

The red *ciervo común* is Europe's largest deer, pre-eminent in the Sierra Morena and the mountains of the south, in the coastal Coto Doñana, and reintroduced into the northern

Above:
Hares are
about twice the size of rabbits and the dark, lean meat has a strong flavour.

Left: Rabbit is so common in Spain that the Romans named the country "rabbit land" – Hispania – from which the modern name is derived.

Cantabrian *cordillera*. Here, you can find all three types of deer: the *ciervo común*, the small *corzo* (roe deer), and the *gamo* (fallow deer). Venison (*venado*) is cooked in wine, roasted or grilled (broiled) and served with a creamy *Cabrales* sauce.

Hare

In Extremadura, hare (*liebre*) is served at engagement parties, the sauce finished with blood, sherry and brandy. It is also often cooked with chocolate. Sometimes it is cooked in the field, in a pot with charcoal on the lid, and accompanied by beans. *Morteruelo*, a pâté of mixed game meats pounded together, is a speciality of Cuenca on the edge of La Mancha.

Rabbit

There are rabbits (*conejos*) all across Spain – so many that the Spanish bred spaniels to chase them. Rabbits are often cooked with snails, which impart the flavour of rosemary, or wild thyme. A Navarran speciality is a pie whose pastry is aromatized by thyme and rosemary. In the south, saffron rice with rabbit is eaten in preference to paella. Rabbit is also cooked with vinegar and garlic (*salmorego*), giving rise to the proverb for a good match – *el salmorejo para el conejo*.

Gathering wild food

Hunters out with a gun and a dog often also collect wild mushrooms, herbs, grubs and snails in their knapsacks – for they are free food. Lizards are caught in Extremadura; the hunters tighten a small noose around the tail of the creature. The lizard's white flesh, which tastes like a cross between a young rabbit and a frog, is eaten in little pots with a tomato sauce. Frogs are a popular food, too, and the hind legs may be battered or fried.

There are many different snails that can be eaten, and they come in all sizes and many flavours. The great black *negros* and *moros* are best grilled (broiled) and eaten with vinegar. The most expensive are the prized Valencia *vaquetas de oliva*; grey and black with a flavour of wild rosemary, upon which they feed. They are commonly added to rice dishes such as paella. In Lérida there is the *caracol de viña* (the same as Burgundy's *petit gris* snail), while in Seville there is the small *caracol* (the generic word for a snail) and the larger *cabrilla*, which means chanterelle, with its pretty whorls of black and white.

Preparing snails

To make an appetizer for four people, you will need about 60 snails. They must be purged before cooking.

1 To purge the snails, put them in a bucket with a weighted lid. After 3 days sprinkle in flour, then leave for another 4 days.

2 The day before cooking, splash the snails with a little fresh water. Discard any that aren't moving. Clean the shells with salt and vinegar, then leave them for 30 minutes before rinsing under cold running water.

3 To cook, put the snails in a pan and cover with warm water, then bring slowly to the boil. Drain, then return to the pan and cover in fresh salted water and bring to the boil again, with a handful of herbs such as wild fennel or bruised parsley stalks. Cook for at least 30 minutes.

4 Drain the snails and add them to a spicy tomato sauce. Simmer for 30 minutes, then serve in individual earthenware dishes. To eat, put a pin into the end, and twist the shell anticlockwise (counterclockwise).

FRUIT AND DESSERTS

More often than not, dessert in Spain is simply a beautifully fragrant piece of fruit. There are only a few true desserts, but they are deeply traditional – and usually incredibly sweet.

FRUIT

Spain is blessed with a huge wealth of fruit. The apricot trees are the first to flower every spring. But it is apples (*manzanas*) that are grown across the country, especially Asturias, with *reinetas* (a Cox type) being a speciality. The orchards of Lérida and Navarra are red with *melocotones* (peaches).

Any Spaniard will boast of the date groves of Elche, of the plums (*ciruelas*) and pears (*peras*), and of the Valle de Jerte that is filled with cherries (*cerezas*). Dark *picota* cherries have no stalks. Quinces are made into a delicious orange paste, *membrillo*, which is often served with cheese. ·

Golden grapes (*uvas*) drape across houses in the south, and the coast from Alicante to Valencia is famous for fat, juicy muscats. They are dried in Málaga as huge black *pasas*. Red-fleshed figs grow wild in the southern scrub, while Granada gained its name from the pomegranate (*granada*). The orange "tomatoes", growing high on bare trees in December, are persimmons (*cakis*).

Below: Pasas de Málaga *are the huge, fat raisins made from muscat grapes.*

Melons (*melones*) have been grown in Spain since the Roman times. The dark-skinned, white-fleshed honeydew melons (*piel de sapo*) are the most highly prized. Strawberries (*fresas*) are another success story. In times past, a train used to run from Madrid to Aranjuez in the summer, carrying picnickers out to the strawberry farms. Now, in Huelva, the strawberries are ripe by Christmas.

Below: Pomegranates are used to make drinks, sorbets and a sauce for chicken.

Above: Spain is renowned for its honeydew melons.

Left: Strawberries are an important Spanish crop.

Citrus fruit

It was the Moors who first planted citrus trees in Spain. The bitter orange came from India in the 11th century, and the juice was squeezed over fish – and still is – in the way we now use lemons. Sweet oranges (*naranjas*) came from China and were planted across the country in the 1550s.

Valencia is the orange capital of Spain and oranges are picked from September to late spring. The small Valencia orange has now been replaced by the seedless Washington navel, and small clementines now represent a quarter of citrus exports. More lemons (*limones*) are grown in Murcia than in Valencia. The summer lemon is the *verna*, with thick peel and juicy flesh, and in winter it is the thin-skinned *fino*.

Tropical fruit

Microclimates allow passion fruit (*pasionara*), loquat (*níspero*) and the custard apple (*cherimoya*) to grow in the south, while in Galicia kiwi and feijoas are cultivated. The Canary Islands are known for a small, sweet banana and the pineapple (*piña*).

Above: Small Valencia oranges have a sweet, tangy, juicy flesh.

FRUIT DESSERTS

Peaches in syrup (*almibar*) are a favourite dessert in Spain, although peaches (or pears) baked whole in red wine are also very popular. Traditional desserts often feature preserved fruit and nuts and are made in winter. Dried figs go into *pan de alá*. The Galicians make superb *marrons glacées* as well as an excellent chestnut and chocolate mousse. They also like freshly roasted chestnuts in a glass of brandy. The Basque Christmas Eve *intxausalsa* is a creamy purée of walnuts.

In Aragón, the crystallized fruit are coated in chocolate. In Cáceres, they make tiny chocolate-coated figs that are out of this world.

MILK PUDDINGS

Custards reign supreme in Spain, and there is a great trio of desserts: *flan* (baked custard), *crema catalana* (crème brûlée) and *tocino de cielo*, which is a baked caramel custard turned out and dark-topped. It looks like an uncut slab of pork, hence its name, which means blissful bacon. Custards (*natilla*) are traditionally made in convents, to sell outside. They may be piled high with *suspiros de mona* (poached meringue); the name means nun's sighs and it is said that the nuns making them sigh regretfully, "Would that I could eat them."

Rice found a sweet niche in the north. The Asturian milk pudding, *arroz con leche*, is flavoured with cinnamon or caramel. Fried custard squares (*leche frita*) are a Basque speciality, and further west pancakes (*filloas*) are popular, served with cream and liqueur. Sugared *flores manchegos* are cooked on special irons and are shaped like flowers. Junket (*cuajada*) and whipped cream (*nata*) are topped with nuts, and *mel y mato* is Catalan cream cheese with honey. Two good cheesecakes are the Santander *quesada*, made with fresh *pasiega*, and the Ibizan *flaó*, which is flavoured with mint.

ICES

The Moors in Granada used to send runners up the mountains to cut ice, even in summer, starting a tradition of *granizados* (grainy iced desserts), made with lemon and sweet fruit syrups (*jarabes*), and later with coffee. The popular frozen dessert today is *tarta helada quemada*, which has a crispy caramel topping.

ALMOND SWEETMEATS

The tradition of serving almond sweetmeats such as *alfajores* (almonds crushed to a paste with honey and wrapped in paper) started in the Moorish harems. *Mazapán* (marzipan) was invented in Toledo when the Moors, besieged by Alfonso VI, ran out of bread and turned to almonds instead. The city now sells little baked half moons of

Honey

Spain specializes in single-flower honey – and there are a great many varieties due to the many mountains, herbs and flowering trees. Valencia is famous for rosemary, *azahar* (citrus blossom) and thyme honeys. Lavender and thyme honeys are produced in the hills behind Córdoba. *Miel de bosque,* from the blossom of Extremeduran oaks, is very dark. Alcarría D.O. is a famous honey centre in Guadalajarra.

Honey is traditionally served with fruit juice, or with almonds or figs, but it is also served with unusual savoury foods such as *bacalao* and *sobrasada* sausage.

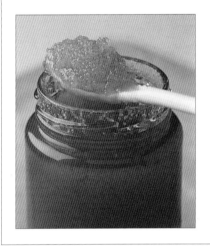

marzipan. *Figuritas de mazapán* are sold at Christmas and you will find them in many different shapes, including little fish, animals, bread shapes, and even miniature musical instruments.

Turrón (nougat) used to be seasonal too, but is now available all year round. In Jijona you can buy a soft almond and honey paste, and in Alicante one with whole marcona almonds embedded in it, while *torta imperiale*, sandwiched between layers of rice paper, is the best in Spain. *Almendras garapiñadas* (crunchy nuts tossed in sweet caramel) are sold at street fairs.

Left: Traditional Spanish sweetmeats date back to the Moorish traditions.

BREAD AND CAKES

Bread is a very important part of the Spanish diet, while cakes and sweet buns are eaten less often than in other countries. Bread shops (*panaderias*) sell bread alone. Cakes and other sweet things are bought from a *pastelería*.

BREAD

As in many European countries, *pan* is Spain's basic food and taken very seriously. Not so long ago consumption was 1kg/2¼lb a head per day. In Galicia, if a piece of bread is dropped, it will be picked up and kissed. It plays a ritual part in weddings, anniversaries and death ceremonies.

Bread accompanies all meals in Spain. It is bought twice a day and eaten very fresh. The *barra* (long loaf) is better, some claim, than French bread. But there are a host of rolls with local names such as *bollas* (balls) and *chicas* (little girls).

Traditional breads

The wheat granary of Spain is the Tierra de Campos in León and south towards Zamora. Here they make the *hogaza* (large loaf) of Castile and the round, white *candeal* bread, which is a classic. In Catalonia, where everything tends to be done slightly differently, the bread is shaped like a three-cornered hat, with slashes across the corners.

Above: Pan de cebada *is a coarse-textured country bread from Galicia, which is exceptional for its barley flour.*

(Salvador Dalí used them to decorate his house.) *Pan cateto* is sourdough bread with a close crumb and chewy crust (*cateto* means country bumpkin); it is dry but long lasting. Bread is also made with pork crackling in it.

Corn meal is used to make corn bread (*pan de maíz*) in Galicia; it is wrapped in leaves and baked overnight in the dying embers of the fire. *Borona* is made with both rye flour and corn meal. Galicians also use bread dough to make their flat two-crust pies, while *bollas preñadas* (pregnant buns) consist of dough folded round sausage meat.

Cocas

Hot from the bread oven, *cocas* are a speciality of the Balearics and Levante. They resemble an Italian pizza but date back much further than that. Once they were just bread dough topped with sardines or salted meat, but today they are spread with tomato sauce, too, and scattered with onions, black olives and herbs. At festival time, there are sweet ones for sale, topped with glistening candied fruit. *Cocarois* are little pastries, folded over with a filling of meat or vegetables.

Using bread

Bread is used in a variety of ways, both in the kitchen and at the table.

Mojado The bread used to scoop up sauced vegetables and seafood tapas.

Rebanada A slice of bread, which is used as a "polite" plate mop at the end of a course.

Pa amb tomàquet Very lightly toasted bread, topped with olive oil and squashed fresh tomato. It is eaten at the start of every meal in Catalonia.

Torrijas These are bread dipped in milk or wine, then fried and sugared.

Migas Breadcrumbs fried in olive oil and a food for all occasions, for every meal and with almost everything. They can be eaten for breakfast after a night on the town, with bacon and eggs; or with fresh fruit as dessert; even with chocolate and sardines – together.

Sobras Yesterday's stale bread is ideal for frying, before being pounded and used to thicken sauces and soups.

Sopa Stale pieces of bread were once common breakfast fare, dunked in coffee, milk and sugar, and eaten with a spoon.

Jam

The best jam is *cabello de angél* (angel's hair) made from the citron melon (*cidra*) which is large and blotched dark green. Jam is used to fill sweet *empanadillas* and cakes, or spread on bread.

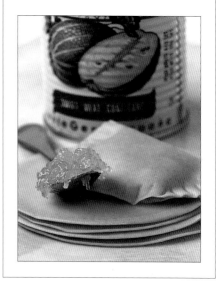

FRITTERS

Dulces de sartén (frying-pan sweets) are the Spanish doughnut, sold on the streets at fairs and in tapas bars. Delicately flavoured with crushed aniseed, and steeped in honey or anis syrup, they betray their Moorish past. *Borrachuelos* are "drunk" on their syrup. Many of them are made in the same way as choux pastry, by beating flour and egg (with wine) in a pan. They may be baked or fried, both of which causes the pastry to puff up.

Plain *empanadillas* (pies) are rolled out with a special rolling pin to stripe the pastry, then sugared; others are filled with angel's hair jam. *Pestiños* (honey-coated fritters) are often hollow – a square folded with opposite corners meeting – to soak up more syrup. *Huesos de santos* (saints' bones) are hollow too, sometimes made of potato dough or almond pastry. *Buñuelos de viento* (*bunyols* in Catalan) are choux puffs, which are eaten on All Saints' Day and at Christmas.

BISCUITS AND COOKIES

Small dry cakes are served with sweet liqueurs, and are often dunked into them. Rings (*rosquillos*) are very common. Many little cookies are made from cinnamon pastry. Others have delightfully descriptive names. S-shaped *mostachones* look like a moustache when two of the cookies are held together; *polverones* (crumble cakes)

Below: Small, dry rosquillos, *made from a wine pastry, are found all over Spain.*

Above: Sobaos pasiegas, from the dairy valley of Pas, are made with butter.

have a powdery texture. *Mantecados*, which are famous in Old Castile, are lardy cookies containing ground almonds. *Macarrones* (macaroons) are made with whisked egg whites and ground almonds, while *almendrados*, made with almonds, and *almori* (honey cakes) reflect the Moorish influence. Moors' sighs (*suspiros de Moros*) are ground almond meringues.

Nuns are traditionally bakers in Old Castile and the south. The nuns of San Leandro in Seville make *yemas* (yolks), whose name describes their colour, shape and content.

LITTLE CAKES AND BUNS

Breakfast is the occasion for some real treats. The melting pastry of Majorcan *ensaimada*, curled like a turban, is also a favourite in Madrid. *Sobaos pasiegas* are rich butter sponges baked in little individual rectangles in papers.

Pan quemado is an all-day Valencian snack. The name means burnt bread, because it is brushed with meringue and sugar before baking, to give it a dark golden crust. For tea time in Madrid, custard-filled puff pastry *bartillos* are eaten. *Medias noches* (midnight buns) are worth sneaking down for at night.

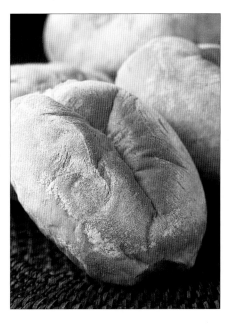

Above: Small, soft bread rolls are good at any time of day.

CAKES

Sponge cakes, made with egg whites only, are light and airy and perfect for soaking up syrups and brandies – as is the tradition in Spain. *Brazo de gitano* (gypsy's arm) is the best-known cake – long and brown and rolled up round *cremadina* (custard). The big traditional cake is *Roscón de Reyes*, an enriched bread-dough ring made for Twelfth Night. It is generously topped with almonds and candied fruit, of which there seems to be more every year.

Below: Simple little magdalenas (butter cakes) *make a delightful treat.*

WINE

There are two great wine styles that are particular to Spain – Rioja and sherry. In Rioja, red wine (but also some white wine) is aged in oak casks, which gives it a light aroma of vanilla. Sherry is a highly sophisticated fortified white wine, and classed with the world's great wines. In Spain, it is drunk as a wine, not just as an aperitif as it is elsewhere.

Spain's viticulture is the largest in the world, and is undergoing a rapid modernization programme. Once behind other countries in technology, Spain's expenditure on modern equipment is resulting in better wines all the time.

Spanish wine drinking is not a very complicated matter. There are no rules about matching food and drink and the Spanish enjoy young wines as well as those that have been aged in oak casks in the traditional way.

RED WINE

Much of Spain's wine is red, with top quality wine produced on the northern rivers and hefty reds with a high alcohol content further south.

Wines on the Ebro river

These are the Riojas; they are soft but not delicate, with a fruity taste. They are blended wines, and some wine firms grow no grapes themselves. Good wines are matured partly in casks, partly in the bottle, which gives an opportunity for a "house taste". Popular brands are San Ascensio made by Campo Viejo, the biggest bodega (wine firm) in Rioja, CUNE and Banda Azul (Blue Stripe) from top exporter Frederick Paternina.

At the expensive end, two traditional houses, Marqués de Murrieta and Marqués de Riscal make big-bodied, oaky reds. With them a newer house in the same style, Marqués de Muga, makes up "the three mighty Ms" of Rioja. However, many modern bodegas favour time maturing in the bottle (not the cask), for example Marqués de Cáceres, Lagunilla and the big exporter Faustino Martínez.

Vintages are important here, as grapes may not always ripen to full potential. There are three regions of Rioja, each with its own distinct style, which will also give clues as to what you are buying. Rioja Baja is low-lying, producing everyday fruity wines. The high Rioja Alta produces wines with more tannin, making them hard and acidic if young, but maturing to a more complex taste. The Rioja Alavesa makes softer, aromatic wines. Part of this region is in Navarra, on the other side of the river, which has a good line in young reds, not unlike Beaujolais.

Wines on the Duero river

Ribera del Duero produces Vega Sicilia, Spain's masterpiece, which is, unfortunately, almost unobtainable. Based on Cabernet Sauvignon, it is aged in casks for ten years or so, and is often 16 years old when sold. Pesquera del Duero is the affordable alternative.

Central Spain

Valdepeñas produces better-quality reds than La Mancha which surrounds it. Huge tinajas (unglazed urns) stand at the roadsides and are used for wine. Here they make aloques, strong but light red wines, and claretes, not claret but a wine of mixed red and white grapes.

The red grapes

Tempranillo is Spain's principal red grape (Ull de Llebre in Catalonia). Used on its own, it makes good, berry-scented young wines, but about 70 per cent of the crop goes into the great Riojas, chiefly supported by the garnacha grape.

Spain's quest for better grapes has been hampered by old D.O. (Denominación de Origen) restrictions. However, new grapes and irrigation, which have been introduced increasingly since the 1960s, have helped to improve quality. Landmarks are the Raimat estate in Costers del Segre, while Jean León introduced Cabernet Sauvignon to Penedès. The palm of honour, however, goes

---

The language of wine
Drinking wine is part of Spanish culture and has its own terms.
Vino de la mesa This is the house wine, usually in una jarra (a jug or pitcher). Una media is a 500ml/ 17fl oz/2¼ cup measure.
Vino corriente This is table wine in its first or second year.
Crianza These wines must be stored for two years after harvest (cosecha). For the first six months the wine is stored in casks, whose oak gives the wine its distinctive flavour. Better quality wines may be held back before they are sold. However, you should beware of five- to six-year-old wines because they may have developed a very oxidized, stale taste.
Reserva This means that the wine has been matured for three years. For whites and rosados (rosé) wines, this means they are in the cask for six months; for reds, this means at least a year, often much more, plus a year in the bottle. Both modest regional wines and good brands carry this label.
Gran reserva This includes much of the best wine, which is only made in fine vintage years or from the best grapes. Cellar-aged for six years, they have at least two years in the cask and three in the bottle – and are splendid value for the quality of wine offered.
Viña This means vineyard, but is a brand not a place. There are few estate-bottled wines.

Right: Campo Viejo is one of the biggest Rioja-producing wine firms in Spain.

to two generations of the Torres family in Penedès, who produce splendid new wines (white, pink and red) with fabulous wines such as Gran Coronas' Black Label, Mas la Plana.

Vast acres of Spain are under vines. La Mancha, with half the vineyards in Spain, produces red wine mainly from the *monastrell* grape. Poor Aragón makes purplish reds, often 15 per cent by volume, because the sun raises alcohol content at the same time as it diminishes quality. Cariñena and Borja in the south-east, and Alicante, Jumilla and Yecla nearer the coast all make hefty reds. Priorato may be Spain's answer to Burgundy. Lighter reds come from Utiel-Requeña and Somontana in the north-east.

PINK WINE

The *rosados* (rosé wines) of Navarra such as Gran Feudo are justly famous, and good ones are made in Aragón, Ribera del Duero, Tarragona and Utiel-Requeña. The cherry-coloured wines, a speciality of Ampurdán, are very good.

WHITE WINE

Good whites are produced on Spain's fringes – north and east – with the masterpiece, sherry, in the south.

Green wine

The *Alberiño* grape produces German-style wines on the slopes of Rías Bajas and Ribera del Duero. Delicately fruity, they give a slight prickle in the mouth and are perfect with shellfish.

Chacoli

The Basques are proud of this wine which they call *txacoli*. It is thin, rather acidic, appley and slightly sparkling.

Rioja whites

White wine is made with the traditional *viura* grape, usually without being aged in the cask. Marqués de Cáceres is a good example of the type. CUNE's Monopole *blanco* is balanced between the two styles, while good oaked examples come from Marqués de Murrieta, Monte Real from Bodegas Riojanas and López de Heredía.

French-style whites

Lighter, fruitier and less alcoholic wines are in demand today, so styles are changing accordingly. New technology is also helping to improve white wines. Typical ones are Antonio Barbadillo in Huelva and Palacio de Bornos, made from the *verdejo* grape, in Rueda.

Whites are a tradition on the north-east coast, with French grapes making French-style wines in the cooler hills. Delicate young whites come from Marqués de Alella just outside Barcelona. Torres makes Viña Sol, which is fresh and slightly lemony (from the Spanish *parellada* grape), Gran Viña Sol (half Chardonnay), or the estate-bottled version, green label, which is matured in oak. Torres' Milmanda is the top Chardonnay in Spain.

South-west Spain

The white wines in the south-west have a strong resemblance to sherry and include *cañamero* and *chiclana*. Most famous, however, is Montilla-Moriles, which has the same nutty scent as sherry, though it is made by conventional methods. Alvear is well-known, especially C.B. (the proprietor's initials), which is the white for cooking.

Sparkling wines

Cavas are wines made by the champagne method in Penedès (although the grapes may come from elsewhere), mainly in San Sadurní de Nova. Codorníu is the largest champagne-style wine producer in the world. Their lovely top-of-the-range wine is the Chardonnay *cava*. Raimat is a good alternative, or Freixenet *cordon negro*, in the black bottle. The Spanish favour sweet *champáns* so do look for "brut" on the label.

Right: Freixenet Cordon Negro is a good quality cava *with a lovely flavour.*

Sherry styles

Fino This is the lightest and driest sherry. It is a pale straw colour.
Manzanilla Meaning camomile, this is similar to *fino*, but has a tang aquired as a result of being stored by the sea.
Amontillado This is matured until it is a soft, dark tawny colour.
Palo cortado This is sweeter still.
Oloroso With more body and a nutty flavour, *olorosos*, as a class, are on the sweet side, sometimes reminiscent of port, but they are also made in dry styles.
Cream sherry This has sweet Pedro Ximénes juice added, which gives it a voluptuous flavour.

Sherry

The name sherry is actually a mispronunciation of the place Jerez de la Frontera. Jerez de la Frontera produces exceptional fortified wines, mainly from the *Palomino* grape, and is one of the few places in Spain with a long tradition of fine wines. Because of its high alcohol content (17 per cent by volume) and the way it is made, it is regarded as an aperitif by the outside world. But in Spain it is a white wine, the natural choice for fish, or a flamenco evening, drunk chilled from the tulip-shaped *copita*, which is never more than two-thirds full. Sherry is made in a *solera* system, a tier of barrels, where the bottom barrels are tapped and the upper barrels are made up with younger wine. The sherry is fortified with brandy, then exposed to air in the cask, where a yeast *flor* grows on the surface to protect it. Darker sherries have oxidized more. Among the great names are Tio Pepe, Barbadillo and Domecq's La Ina.

SOUP AND EGGS

Gazpacho is the world-famous Spanish soup but there are many others, from a hearty shellfish soup to a rich ham-scented broth with beans. Tortilla is another classic dish identified with Spain, and eggs hold a special place in the Spanish heart — they speak of the barnyard, and the country, where every Spaniard yearns to live.

GAZPACHO

THIS CLASSIC CHILLED SOUP IS DEEPLY ROOTED IN ANDALUSIA. THE SOOTHING BLEND OF TOMATOES, SWEET PEPPERS AND GARLIC IS SHARPENED WITH SHERRY VINEGAR, AND ENRICHED WITH OLIVE OIL. SERVING IT WITH SAUCERFULS OF GARNISHES HAS VIRTUALLY BECOME A TRADITION.

SERVES FOUR

INGREDIENTS

1.3–1.6kg/3–3½lb ripe tomatoes
1 green (bell) pepper, seeded and
    roughly chopped
2 garlic cloves, finely chopped
2 slices stale bread, crusts removed
60ml/4 tbsp extra virgin olive oil
60ml/4 tbsp sherry vinegar
150ml/¼ pint/⅔ cup tomato juice
300ml/½ pint/1¼ cups iced water
salt and ground black pepper
ice cubes, to serve (optional)
For the garnishes
30ml/2 tbsp olive oil
2–3 slices stale bread, diced
1 small cucumber, peeled
    and finely diced
1 small onion, finely chopped
1 red (bell) and 1 green (bell)
    pepper, seeded and finely diced
2 hard-boiled eggs, chopped

COOK'S TIP
In Spain, ripe tomatoes are used for salads and very ripe ones for sauces and soups. No further flavouring ingredients are needed. If you cannot find really ripe tomatoes, add a pinch of sugar to sweeten the soup slightly.

1 Skin the tomatoes, then quarter them and remove the cores and seeds, saving the juices. Put the pepper in a food processor and process for a few seconds. Add the tomatoes, reserved juices, garlic, bread, oil and vinegar and process. Add the tomato juice and blend to combine.

2 Season the soup, then pour into a large bowl, cover with clear film (plastic wrap) and chill for at least 12 hours.

3 Prepare the garnishes. Heat the olive oil in a frying pan and fry the bread cubes for 4–5 minutes until golden brown and crisp. Drain well on kitchen paper, then arrange in a small dish. Place each of the remaining garnishes in separate small dishes.

4 Just before serving, dilute the soup with the ice-cold water. The consistency should be thick but not too stodgy. If you like, stir a few ice cubes into the soup, then spoon into serving bowls and serve with the garnishes.

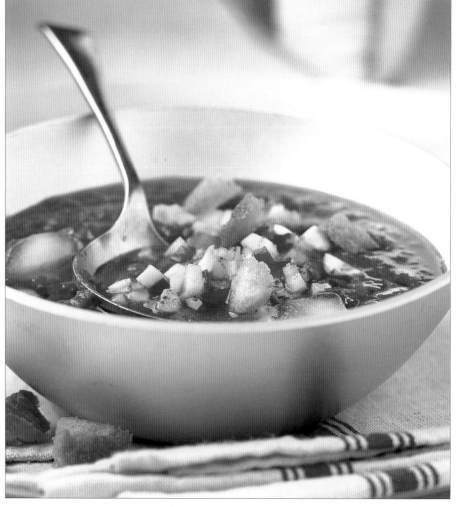

CHILLED AVOCADO SOUP WITH CUMIN

ANDALUSIA IS HOME TO BOTH AVOCADOS AND GAZPACHO, SO IT IS NOT SURPRISING THAT THIS CHILLED AVOCADO SOUP, WHICH IS ALSO KNOWN AS GREEN GAZPACHO, WAS INVENTED THERE. IN SPAIN, THIS DELICIOUSLY MILD, CREAMY SOUP IS KNOWN AS SOPA DE AGUACATE.

SERVES FOUR

INGREDIENTS

3 ripe avocados
1 bunch spring onions (scallions), white parts only, trimmed and roughly chopped
2 garlic cloves, chopped
juice of 1 lemon
1.5ml/¼ tsp ground cumin
1.5ml/¼ tsp paprika
450ml/¾ pint/scant 2 cups fresh chicken stock, cooled, and all fat skimmed off
300ml/½ pint/1¼ cups iced water
salt and ground black pepper
roughly chopped fresh flat leaf parsley, to serve

1 Starting half a day ahead, put the flesh of one avocado in a food processor or blender. Add the spring onions, garlic and lemon juice and purée until smooth. Add the second avocado and purée, then the third, with the spices and seasoning. Purée until smooth.

2 Gradually add the chicken stock. Pour the soup into a metal bowl and chill.

3 To serve, stir in the iced water, then season to taste with plenty of salt and black pepper. Garnish with chopped parsley and serve immediately.

CHILLED ALMOND SOUP <u>WITH</u> GRAPES

CALLED AJO BLANCO — WHITE GARLIC SOUP — IN SPAIN, THIS IS A CHILLED MOORISH SOUP OF ANCIENT ORIGIN. IT IS A PERFECT BALANCE OF THREE SOUTHERN INGREDIENTS: CRUSHED ALMONDS, GARLIC AND VINEGAR, IN A SMOOTH PURÉE MADE LUSCIOUS WITH OIL.

SERVES SIX

INGREDIENTS
   115g/4oz stale white bread
   115g/4oz/1 cup blanched
     almonds
   2 garlic cloves, sliced
   75ml/5 tbsp olive oil
   25ml/1½ tbsp sherry vinegar
   salt and ground black pepper
For the garnish
   toasted flaked almonds
   green and black grapes, halved
     and seeded
   chopped fresh chives

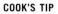

1 Break the bread into a bowl and pour in 150ml/¼ pint/⅔ cup cold water. Leave to soak for about 5 minutes, then squeeze dry.

2 Put the almonds and garlic in a food processor or blender and process until very finely ground. Add the soaked white bread and process again until thoroughly combined.

3 Continue to process, gradually adding the oil until the mixture forms a smooth paste. Add the sherry vinegar, followed by 600ml/1 pint/ 2½ cups cold water and process until the mixture is smooth.

4 Transfer the soup to a bowl and season with plenty of salt and pepper, adding a little more water if the soup is very thick. Cover with clear film (plastic wrap) and chill for at least 2 hours.

5 Ladle the soup into bowls. Scatter the almonds, halved grapes and chopped chives over to garnish.

COOK'S TIP
To accentuate the flavour of the almonds, dry roast them in a frying pan until they are lightly browned before grinding them. This will produce a slightly darker soup.

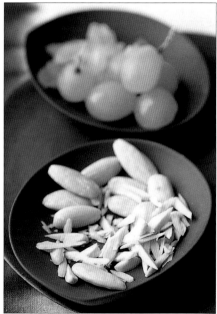

SHERRIED ONION SOUP <u>WITH</u> SAFFRON

*THE SPANISH COMBINATION OF ONIONS, SHERRY AND SAFFRON GIVES THIS PALE YELLOW SOUP A
BEGUILING FLAVOUR THAT IS PERFECT FOR THE OPENING COURSE OF A MEAL. THE ADDITION OF
GROUND ALMONDS TO THICKEN THE SOUP GIVES IT A WONDERFUL TEXTURE AND FLAVOUR.*

SERVES FOUR

INGREDIENTS

   40g/1½oz/3 tbsp butter
   2 large yellow onions, thinly sliced
   1 small garlic clove, finely chopped
   pinch of saffron threads (0.05g)
   50g/2oz blanched almonds, toasted
    and finely ground
   750ml/1¼ pints/3 cups chicken
    or vegetable stock
   45ml/3 tbsp fino sherry
   2.5ml/½ tsp paprika
   salt and ground black pepper
To garnish
   30ml/2 tbsp flaked or slivered
    almonds, toasted
   chopped fresh parsley

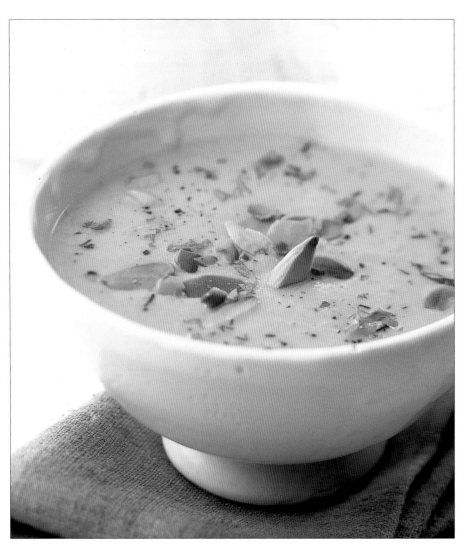

1 Melt the butter in a heavy pan over
a low heat. Add the onions and garlic,
stirring to ensure that they are
thoroughly coated in the melted butter,
then cover the pan and cook very
gently, stirring frequently, for about
20 minutes, or until the onions are
soft and golden yellow.

2 Add the saffron threads to the pan
and cook, uncovered, for 3–4 minutes,
then add the finely ground almonds and
cook, stirring the ingredients constantly,
for a further 2–3 minutes.

3 Pour in the chicken or vegetable
stock and sherry into the pan and stir in
5ml/1 tsp salt and the paprika. Season
with plenty of black pepper. Bring to the
boil, then lower the heat and simmer
gently for about 10 minutes.

4 Pour the soup into a food processor
and process until smooth, then return it
to the rinsed pan. Reheat slowly, without
allowing the soup to boil, stirring
occasionally. Taste for seasoning, adding
more salt and pepper if required.

5 Ladle the soup into heated bowls,
garnish with the toasted flaked or
slivered almonds and a little chopped
fresh parsley and serve immediately.

VARIATION

This soup is also delicious served chilled.
Use olive oil rather than butter, add a
little more chicken or vegetable stock to
make a slightly thinner soup, then leave
to cool and chill for at least 4 hours.
Just before serving, taste for seasoning.
(Chilled soups need more seasoning than
hot ones.) Float one or two ice cubes in
each bowl, then garnish with almonds
and parsley and serve immediately.

SOPA DE MARISCOS

This hearty seafood soup contains all the colours and flavours of the Mediterranean. It is substantial enough to serve as a main course, but can also be diluted with a little white wine and water, to make an elegant appetizer for six.

SERVES FOUR

INGREDIENTS

675g/1½lb raw prawns (shrimp), in the shell
900ml/1½pints/3¾ cups cold water
1 onion, chopped
1 celery stick, chopped
1 bay leaf
45ml/3 tbsp olive oil
2 slices stale bread, crusts removed
1 small onion, finely chopped
1 large garlic clove, chopped
2 large tomatoes, halved
½ large green (bell) pepper, finely chopped
500g/1¼lb cockles (small clams) or mussels, cleaned
juice of 1 lemon
45ml/3 tbsp chopped fresh parsley
5ml/1 tsp paprika
salt and ground black pepper

COOK'S TIP
Good fish and shellfish dishes are normally based on proper fish stock (including the juices saved from opening mussels). This is equivalent to the French *court bouillon*, and takes 30 minutes' simmering. The method used here is one of the quickest, because the prawn heads come off neatly, and the rest of the shells are simply added as they are removed.

1 Pull the heads off the prawns and put them in a pan with the cold water. Add the onion, celery and bay leaf and simmer for 20–25 minutes.

2 Peel the prawns, adding the shells to the stock as you go along.

3 Heat the oil in a wide, deep flameproof casserole and fry the bread slices quickly, then reserve them. Fry the onion until it is soft, adding the garlic towards the end.

4 Scoop the seeds out of the tomatoes and discard. Chop the flesh and add to the casserole with the green pepper. Fry briefly, stirring occasionally.

5 Strain the stock into the casserole and bring to the boil. Check over the cockles or mussels, discarding any that are open or damaged.

6 Add half the cockles or mussels to the stock. When open, use a slotted spoon to transfer some of them out on to a plate. Remove the mussels or cockles from the shells and discard the shells. (You should end up having discarded about half of the shells.) Meanwhile, repeat the process to cook the remaining cockles or mussels.

7 Return the cockles or mussels to the soup and add the prawns. Add the bread, torn into little pieces, and the lemon juice and chopped parsley.

8 Season to taste with paprika, salt and pepper and stir gently to dissolve the bread. Serve at once in soup bowls, providing a plate for the empty shells.

SOPA CASTILIANA

THIS RICH, DARK GARLIC SOUP, FROM CENTRAL SPAIN, DIVIDES PEOPLE INTO TWO GROUPS. YOU EITHER LOVE IT OR HATE IT. THE PITILESS SUN BEATS DOWN ON LA MANCHA, ONE OF THE POOREST REGIONS OF SPAIN, AND THE LOCAL SOUP HAS HARSH, STRONG TASTES TO MATCH THE CLIMATE. POACHING A WHOLE EGG IN EACH BOWL JUST BEFORE SERVING TRANSFORMS THE SOUP INTO A MEAL.

SERVES FOUR

INGREDIENTS
   30ml/2 tbsp olive oil
   4 large garlic cloves, peeled
   4 slices stale country bread
   20ml/4 tbsp paprika
   1 litre/1¾ pints/4 cups beef stock
   1.5ml/¼ tsp ground cumin
   4 free-range (farm-fresh) eggs
   salt and ground black pepper
   chopped fresh parsley, to garnish

VARIATION
If you prefer, you can simply whisk the eggs into the hot soup.

1 Preheat the oven to 230°C/450°F/ Gas 8. Heat the olive oil in a large pan. Add the whole peeled garlic cloves and cook until they are golden, then remove and set aside. Fry the slices of bread in the oil until golden, then set these aside.

2 Add 15ml/1 tbsp of the paprika to the pan, and fry for a few seconds. Stir in the beef stock, cumin and remaining paprika, then add the reserved garlic, crushing the cloves with the back of a wooden spoon. Season to taste, then cook for about 5 minutes.

3 Break up the slices of fried bread into bitesize pieces and stir them into the soup. Ladle the soup into four ovenproof bowls. Carefully break an egg into each bowl of soup and place in the oven for about 3 minutes, until the eggs are set. Sprinkle the soup with chopped fresh parsley and serve immediately.

CALDO GALLEGO

THIS CLASSIC GALICIAN SOUP FEATURES SALT PORK AND BEANS WITH YOUNG TURNIP TOPS, ALTHOUGH PURPLE SPROUTING BROCCOLI MAKES A PRETTY SUBSTITUTE. MAKE THE SOUP AHEAD OF TIME, THEN LET THE FLAVOURS BLEND. YOU WILL NEED TO START MAKING THE SOUP AT LEAST A DAY IN ADVANCE.

SERVES SIX

INGREDIENTS

150g/5oz/⅔ cup haricot beans,
    soaked overnight in cold water
    and drained
1kg/2¼lb smoked gammon (cured
    or smoked ham) hock
3 potatoes, quartered
3 small turnips, sliced in rounds
150g/5oz purple sprouting broccoli
salt and ground black pepper

1 Put the drained beans and gammon into a casserole and cover with 2 litres/3½ pints/8 cups water. Slowly bring to the boil, skim off any scum, then turn down the heat and cook gently, covered, for about 1¼ hours.

2 Drain, reserving the broth. Return the broth to the casserole and add the potatoes, turnips and drained beans.

3 Meanwhile, strip all the gammon off the bone and return the bone to the broth. Discard the rind, fat and gristle and chop half the meat coarsely. Reserve the remaining meat for another recipe.

4 Add the chopped meat to the casserole. Discard the hard stalks from the broccoli and add the leaves and florets to the broth. Simmer for 10 minutes. Season generously with pepper, then remove the bone and leave the soup to stand for at least half a day.

5 To serve, reheat the soup, add a little more seasoning if necessary, and ladle into soup bowls.

COOK'S TIP
The leftover gammon can be chopped into bitesize pieces and added to rice or vegetable dishes, or tortillas.

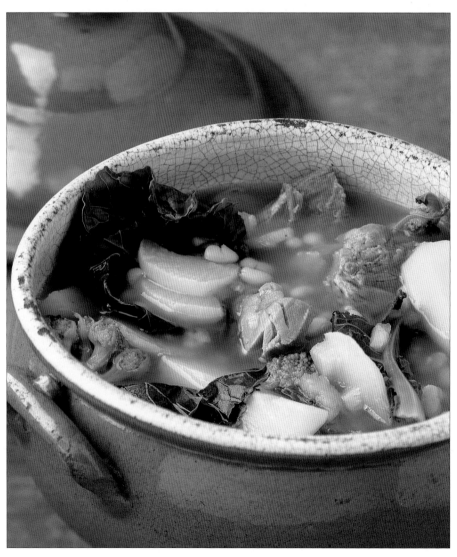

POTATO TORTILLA

THE CLASSIC TORTILLA STANDS ON EVERY TAPAS BAR IN SPAIN. THE SIZE OF A LARGE CAKE, IT IS DENSE AND VERY SATISFYING. IT CAN BE EATEN IN WEDGES WITH A FORK — A MEAL IN ITSELF WITH SALAD — OR CUT UP INTO CHUNKS AND SPEARED, TO BE ENJOYED AS A SNACK WITH DRINKS.

SERVES SIX

INGREDIENTS
    450g/1lb small waxy potatoes, peeled
    1 Spanish onion
    45ml/3 tbsp vegetable oil
    4 large (US extra large) eggs
    salt and ground black pepper
    fresh flat leaf parsley or tomato
        wedges, to garnish

1 Using a sharp knife, cut the potatoes into thin slices and slice the onion into thin rings. Heat 30ml/2 tbsp of the oil in a 20cm/8in heavy frying pan.

2 Add the potatoes and the onions to the pan and cook over a low heat for 20 minutes, or until the potato slices are just tender. Remove from the heat.

3 In a large bowl, beat together the eggs with a little salt and pepper. Stir in the cooked potatoes and onion.

4 Clean the frying pan with kitchen paper then heat the remaining oil and pour in the potato mixture. Cook very gently for 5–8 minutes until set underneath. During cooking, lift the edges of the tortilla with a spatula, and allow any uncooked egg to run underneath. Shake the pan from side to side, to prevent sticking.

5 Place a large heatproof plate upside-down over the pan, invert the tortilla on to the plate and then slide it back into the pan. Cook for 2–3 minutes more, until the underside of the tortilla is golden brown. Cut into wedges and serve, garnished with fresh flat leaf parsley or tomato wedges.

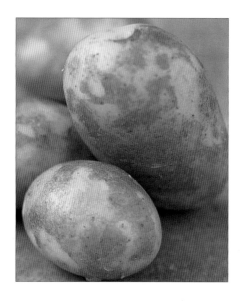

PAN-FRIED HAM <u>AND</u> VEGETABLES <u>WITH</u> EGGS

LITTLE VEGETABLE DISHES, AND ONES THAT CONTAIN HAM OR EGGS, OR BOTH, ARE THE BACKBONE OF THE SPANISH SUPPER SCENE. THIS DELICIOUS DISH IS INCREDIBLY SIMPLE TO MAKE AND IS HEARTY ENOUGH TO SERVE AS A MEAL IN ITSELF. UNLIKE TORTILLA, THE EGGS ARE NOT BEATEN, BUT ARE BROKEN INTO THE VEGETABLE MIXTURE AND COOKED WHOLE.

SERVES FOUR

INGREDIENTS
 30ml/2 tbsp olive oil
 1 onion, roughly chopped
 2 garlic cloves, finely chopped
 175g/6oz cooked ham
 225g/8oz courgettes (zucchini)
 1 red (bell) pepper, seeded and
   thinly sliced
 1 yellow (bell) pepper, seeded
   and thinly sliced
 10ml/2 tsp paprika
 400g/14oz can chopped tomatoes
 15ml/1 tbsp sun-dried tomato
   purée (paste)
 4 large (US extra large) eggs
 115g/4oz/1 cup coarsely grated
   Cheddar cheese
 salt and ground black pepper
 crusty bread, to serve

1 Heat the olive oil in a deep frying pan. Add the onion and garlic and cook for 4 minutes, stirring frequently.

2 Meanwhile, cut the cooked ham and courgettes into 5cm/2in batons.

3 Add the courgettes and peppers to the pan and cook over a medium heat for 3–4 minutes.

4 Stir in the paprika, tomatoes, tomato purée, ham and seasoning. Bring to a simmer and cook gently for 15 minutes.

5 Reduce the heat to low. Make four wells in the tomato mixture, break an egg into each and season. Cook over a gentle heat until the white begins to set. Preheat the grill (broiler). Sprinkle the cheese over and grill (broil) for about 5 minutes until the eggs are set.

SALADS AND VEGETABLES

Salads start the meal in summer, and are typical of Spain's attitude to cooking, using fresh, local seasonal ingredients. Vegetable dishes are inventive too, eaten as a course on their own, or perhaps as a supper. Simple ingredients are cleverly paired to show off their qualities to perfection.

ORANGE AND RED ONION SALAD WITH CUMIN

DURING WINTER IN THE SOUTH OF SPAIN, WHEN OTHER SALAD INGREDIENTS ARE IN SHORT SUPPLY, ORANGES OFTEN FORM THE BASIS OF SALADS. IN THIS ENSALADA DE NARANJAS *THEY ARE PARTNERED WITH THINLY SLICED RED ONIONS AND BLACK OLIVES, AND FLAVOURED WITH TWO POPULAR MIDDLE EASTERN INGREDIENTS — CUMIN SEEDS AND MINT.*

SERVES SIX

INGREDIENTS
   6 oranges
   2 red onions
   15ml/1 tbsp cumin seeds
   5ml/1 tsp coarsely ground
      black pepper
   15ml/1 tbsp chopped fresh mint
   90ml/6 tbsp olive oil
   salt
   fresh mint sprigs and black olives,
      to garnish

COOK'S TIP
It is important to let the salad stand before serving. This allows the flavours to develop and the pungent taste of the onion to soften slightly.

1 Using a sharp knife, slice the oranges thinly, working over a bowl to catch any juice. Then, holding each orange slice in turn over the bowl, cut round the middle fleshy section with scissors to remove the peel and pith. Reserve the juice. Slice the two red onions thinly and separate the rings.

2 Arrange the orange and onion slices in layers in a shallow dish, sprinkling each layer with cumin seeds, pepper, mint, olive oil and salt. Pour in the reserved orange juice. Leave to marinate in a cool place for about 2 hours. Just before serving, scatter with the mint sprigs and black olives.

MIXED SALAD WITH OLIVES AND CAPERS

COLOURFUL SALADS START MANY SUMMER MEALS IN SPAIN, AND ARE A COMMUNAL AFFAIR. THE BOWL IS PUT IN THE CENTRE OF THE TABLE AND EVERYONE HELPS THEMSELVES, WITH A FORK.

SERVES FOUR

INGREDIENTS
   4 large tomatoes
   ½ cucumber
   1 bunch spring onions (scallions)
   1 bunch watercress or rocket
      (arugula), washed
   8 pimiento-stuffed olives
   30ml/2 tbsp drained pickled capers
For the dressing
   1 garlic clove, finely chopped
   30ml/2 tbsp red wine vinegar
   5ml/1 tsp paprika
   2.5ml/½ tsp ground cumin
   75ml/5 tbsp virgin olive oil
   salt and ground black pepper

COOK'S TIP
In Spain, tomatoes are always used when red and ripe. Firm tomatoes should be used in salads and soft ones in sauces.

1 To peel the tomatoes, place them in a heatproof bowl, pour over boiling water to cover and leave to stand for 1 minute. Lift out with a slotted spoon and plunge into a bowl of cold water. Leave for 1 minute, then drain. Slip off the skins and dice the flesh finely. Put in a salad bowl.

2 Peel the cucumber, dice finely and add to the tomatoes. Trim and chop half the spring onions, and add to the bowl.

3 Toss the vegetables together, then break the watercress or rocket into small sprigs. Add to the tomato mixture, with the olives and capers.

4 Make the dressing. Crush the garlic to a paste with a little salt, using the flat of a knife. Put in a bowl and mix in the vinegar and spices. Whisk in the oil and taste for seasoning. Dress the salad, and serve garnished with the remaining spring onions.

MUSHROOM, BEAN AND CHORIZO SALAD

THIS REALLY SIMPLE SALAD CAN BE SERVED AS AN ACCOMPANIMENT TO PLAIN FISH OR CHICKEN DISHES, OR SERVED WITH CRUSTY BREAD AS A HEARTY LUNCH OR SUPPER DISH. THE COMBINATION OF SPICY SAUSAGE, TENDER, SWEET BEANS AND DELICATE MUSHROOMS IS QUITE DELICIOUS.

SERVES FOUR

INGREDIENTS
  225g/8oz shelled broad (fava) beans
  175g/6oz frying chorizo
  60ml/4 tbsp extra virgin olive oil
  225g/8oz/3 cups brown cap (cremini)
    mushrooms, sliced
  60ml/4 tbsp chopped fresh chives
  salt and ground black pepper

COOK'S TIP
Although peeling the skins from broad beans can be time consuming, it is well worth it. Beans with tough, bitter skins will spoil the delicate taste and texture of this lovely salad.

1 Cook the broad beans in a pan of salted boiling water for 7–8 minutes. Drain and refresh under cold water.

2 Remove the skin from the sausage. If it doesn't peel off easily, score along the length of the sausage with a sharp knife first. Cut the chorizo into small chunks. Heat the oil in a small pan, add the chorizo and cook for 2–3 minutes.

3 Put the sliced mushrooms in a bowl and tip in the chorizo and oil. Toss to combine then leave to cool.

4 If the beans are large, peel away the tough outer skins. Stir the beans and half the chives into the mushroom mixture, and season to taste. Serve at room temperature, garnished with the remaining chives.

AVOCADO, ORANGE AND ALMOND SALAD

IN ANDALUSIA, AVOCADOS HAVE BECOME ONE OF THE BIG CASH CROPS, REPLACING MANY ORANGE ORCHARDS. IN THIS SALAD, ENSALADA DE AGUACATES, *THE SMOOTH, CREAMY AVOCADOS COMBINE PERFECTLY WITH LOCALLY GROWN ORANGES AND ALMONDS.*

SERVES FOUR

INGREDIENTS
  2–3 oranges
  2 ripe tomatoes
  2 small avocados
  60ml/4 tbsp extra virgin olive oil
  30ml/2 tbsp lemon juice
  15ml/1 tbsp chopped fresh parsley
  small onion rings
  25g/1oz/¼ cup split, toasted
    almonds
  10–12 black olives
  salt and ground black pepper

COOK'S TIP
Spanish onions are sweet and mild, and pleasant to eat raw, but they are very large. Slice them and use just the small central rings for salads, keeping the large outer rings for frying.

1 Peel the oranges and slice them into thick rounds. Plunge the tomatoes into boiling water for 30 seconds, then refresh in cold water. Peel away the skins, cut the tomatoes into quarters, remove the seeds and chop roughly.

2 Cut the avocados in half, remove the stones and carefully peel away the skin. Cut into chunks.

3 Mix together the olive oil, lemon juice and parsley. Season with salt and pepper, then toss the avocados and tomatoes in half of the dressing.

4 Arrange the sliced oranges on a plate and scatter with the onion rings. Drizzle with the remaining dressing. Spoon the avocados, tomatoes, almonds and olives on top and serve immediately.

STUFFED TOMATOES AND PEPPERS

COLOURFUL PEPPERS AND TOMATOES MAKE PERFECT CONTAINERS FOR A SIMPLE RICE, NUT AND HERB STUFFING. THE VEGETABLES BECOME DELICIOUSLY SWEET AND JUICY WHEN BAKED. SERVE TOMATOES Y PIMIENTAS RELLENOS AS A SUBSTANTIAL STARTER OR A SUPPER DISH.

3 Halve the peppers, leaving the cores intact. Scoop out the seeds. Brush the peppers with 15ml/1 tbsp of the oil.

4 Fry the onions and garlic in 30ml/ 2 tbsp oil. Stir in most of the almonds. Add the rice, tomato pulp, drained raisins, mint and 30ml/2 tbsp parsley. Season well, then spoon the mixture into the vegetable cases.

5 Bake uncovered for 20 minutes. Finely chop the remaining almonds and parsley in a food processor and sprinkle over the top. Drizzle with 15–30ml/ 1–2 tbsp olive oil. Return to the oven and bake for a further 20 minutes, or until turning golden. Serve, garnished with more chopped parsley if wished.

SERVES FOUR

INGREDIENTS
  2 large tomatoes
  1 green (bell) pepper
  1 yellow or orange (bell) pepper
  75ml/5 tbsp olive oil
  2 onions, finely chopped
  2 garlic cloves, finely chopped
  75g/3 oz/¾ cup almonds, chopped
  175g/6oz/1½ cups cooked rice, or
    75g/3oz/scant ½ cup long grain
    rice, cooked and drained
  30ml/2 tbsp Malaga raisins or
    muscatels, soaked in hot water
  30ml/2 tbsp chopped fresh mint
  45ml/3 tbsp chopped fresh flat
    leaf parsley
  salt and ground pepper

1 Preheat the oven to 190°C/375°F/ Gas 5. Cut the tomatoes in half and scoop out the pulp and seeds.

2 Put the tomato halves on kitchen paper with the cut sides down and leave to drain. Roughly chop the centres and seeds and place in a bowl.

VARIATION
Small aubergines (eggplant) or large courgettes (zucchini) are also good stuffed. Scoop out the centres, then oil the vegetable cases and bake for about 15 minutes. Chop the centres, fry to soften and add to the stuffing mixture, then fill and bake as for the peppers and tomatoes.

STEWED AUBERGINE

THE ARABS INTRODUCED THIS STRANGE VEGETABLE-FRUIT TO ANDALUSIA, WHERE IT WAS COOKED WITH THE ARAB FLAVOURINGS OF CUMIN AND GARLIC. LATER, DISHES SIMILAR TO FRENCH RATATOUILLE BECAME POPULAR. THIS IS A MODERN VERSION OF BERENJENA GUISADA, WITH RED WINE.

SERVES FOUR

INGREDIENTS
1 large aubergine (eggplant)
60–90ml/4–6 tbsp olive oil
2 shallots, thinly sliced
4 tomatoes, quartered
2 garlic cloves, thinly sliced
60ml/4 tbsp red wine
30ml/2 tbsp chopped fresh parsley,
  plus extra to garnish
30–45ml/2–3 tbsp virgin olive oil
  (if serving cold)
salt and ground black pepper

3 Heat 30ml/2 tbsp of the oil in a large frying pan until smoking. Add one layer of aubergine slices and fry, turning once, until golden brown. Remove to a plate covered with kitchen paper. Heat more oil and fry the second batch in the same way.

4 Heat 15ml/1 tbsp of oil in a pan and cook the shallots for 5 minutes until golden. Cut the aubergine into strips. Add, with the tomatoes, garlic and wine. Cover and simmer for 30 minutes.

5 Stir in the parsley, and check the seasonings. Sprinkle with a little more parsley and serve hot. To serve cold, dribble a little virgin olive oil over the dish before it goes on the table.

COOK'S TIP
Be sure to heat the oil before adding the aubergine slices and do not be tempted to add more oil once the aubergines are cooking. They will absorb cold oil, resulting in a greasy dish.

1 Slice the aubergine into 1cm/½in rounds. Place them in a large colander and sprinkle with 5–10ml/1–2 tsp salt. Leave to drain for 30 minutes.

2 Rinse the aubergine slices well, then press between several layers of kitchen paper to remove any excess liquid.

MENESTRA

THIS VEGETABLE DISH, WHICH CONTAINS AN ASSORTMENT OF YOUNG, NEW VEGETABLES, IS EATEN ALL ALONG THE NORTHERN COAST OF SPAIN TO CELEBRATE THE ARRIVAL OF SPRING. CHOOSE BY EYE, KEEPING THE QUANTITIES IN PROPORTION, AND PAYING CAREFUL ATTENTION TO THE COOKING TIME EACH VEGETABLE REQUIRES TO STAY JUST CRISP.

SERVES SIX

INGREDIENTS
   15ml/1 tbsp olive oil
   115g/4oz streaky (fatty) bacon
      lardons or diced pancetta
   1 onion, chopped
   3 garlic cloves, finely chopped
   90ml/6 tbsp chopped fresh parsley
   175ml/6fl oz/¾ cup dry white wine
   150g/5oz green beans
   200g/7oz bunched young carrots
   6 small new best potatoes, scrubbed
   300ml/10fl oz/1¼ cups
      chicken stock
   1 corn cob, kernels removed
      (optional)
   200g/7oz/2 cups peas
   50g/2oz mangetout (snow peas)
   salt and ground black pepper
   2 hard-boiled eggs, chopped,
      to garnish

VARIATION
Change the vegetables at will – the stalk end of asparagus, for example, is excellent. But don't vary the amount of liquid used in the casserole, or the sauce will become watery.

1 Heat the oil in a small flameproof casserole and fry the bacon or pancetta over a gentle heat for about 5 minutes, or until it crisps. Remove with a slotted spoon and reserve. Add the onion to the casserole and cook in the bacon fat until softened, adding the garlic towards the end.

2 Remove the cooked onion to a food processor, add 30ml/2 tbsp of the chopped parsley and purée with a little of the white wine.

3 Meanwhile prepare all the vegetables. Cut the beans into short lengths, and the carrots to the same size.

4 Bring a pan of salted water to the boil and add the potatoes. Cook for about 10 minutes. Add the carrots to the pan of potatoes, and cook for a further 5 minutes.

5 Meanwhile, return the bacon to the casserole and add the stock. Put in the green beans, corn and peas and lay the mangetout over the top. Half cover the casserole and leave it to simmer for 5–10 minutes, until the vegetables are just cooked.

6 Drain the potatoes and carrots and add them to the casserole.

7 Add the rest of the wine and the onion purée to the casserole, warming the liquid and turning the vegetables gently with a wooden spoon. Check the seasoning, adding more if necessary, and serve with the juices. Garnish with chopped egg and the remaining parsley.

VARIATION
This dish can also be made with tender meats such as lamb and veal with various combinations of new vegetables. Good combinations include lamb with artichokes and sherry, and veal with carrots and peas. Chop the meat and fry before adding to the casserole with the vegetables for further cooking.

PISTO MANCHEGO

A RICH-FLAVOURED AND SIMPLE SUMMER VEGETABLE DISH, FROM THE POOREST AND HOTTEST PART OF SPAIN, LA MANCHA. IT MAY BE EATEN HOT, ALONE OR WITH SUCH THINGS AS FRIED HAM AND EGGS. IT ALSO MAKES A SUBSTANTIAL SALAD, OFTEN WITH CANNED TUNA, OR HARD-BOILED EGGS.

SERVES FOUR

INGREDIENTS

45–60ml/3–4 tbsp olive oil
2 Spanish (Bermuda) onions, thinly sliced
3 garlic cloves, finely chopped
3 large green (bell) peppers, seeded and chopped
3 large courgettes (zucchini), thinly sliced
5 large ripe tomatoes or 800g/ 1¾lb canned tomatoes, with juice
60ml/4 tbsp chopped fresh parsley
2 hard-boiled eggs (optional)
30–45ml/2–3 tbsp virgin olive oil (if serving cold)
salt and ground black pepper

1 Heat the oil in a large heavy pan or flameproof casserole and cook the onions and garlic gently, until soft.

2 Add the peppers, courgettes and tomatoes. Season and cook gently for 20 minutes until the flavours blend.

3 Stir in 30ml/2 tbsp parsley and serve hot, if you wish, topped with chopped hard-boiled egg, if using, and more parsley. To serve cold, check the seasoning, adding more if needed, and sprinkle with a little virgin olive oil before adding the garnish.

ESCALIVADA

The Catalan name of this celebrated dish means "baked over embers" and, like many other barbecue dishes, it transfers very successfully to the oven. Cooking the vegetables in this way brings out their flavour magnificently.

SERVES FOUR

INGREDIENTS

    2–3 courgettes (zucchini)
    1 large fennel bulb
    1 Spanish (Bermuda) onion
    2 large red (bell) peppers
    450g/1lb butternut squash
    6 whole garlic cloves, unpeeled
    75ml/5 tbsp olive oil
    juice of ½ lemon
    pinch of cumin seeds, crushed
    4 sprigs fresh thyme
    4 medium tomatoes
    salt and ground black pepper

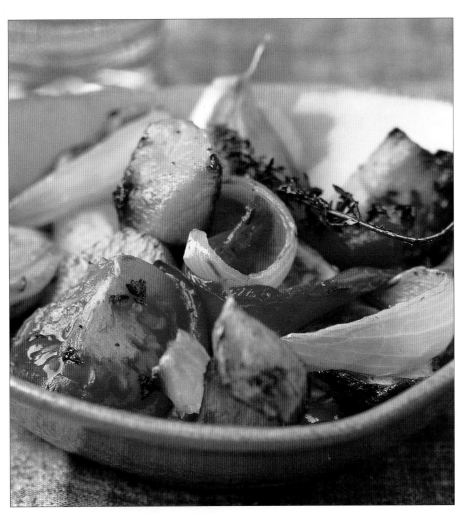

1 Preheat the oven to 220°C/425°F/ Gas 7. Cut the courgettes lengthways into four pieces. Cut the fennel into similar-sized wedges. Slice the onion lengthways into chunks. Halve and seed the peppers, and slice thickly lengthways. Cut the squash into thick chunks. Smash the garlic cloves with the flat of a knife, but leave the skins on.

2 Choose a roasting pan into which all the vegetables will fit in one layer. Put in all the vegetables except the tomatoes. Mix together the oil and lemon juice. Pour over the vegetables and toss them. Sprinkle with the cumin seeds, salt and pepper and tuck in the thyme sprigs. Roast for 20 minutes.

3 Gently stir the vegetables in the oil and add the tomatoes. Cook for a further 15 minutes, or until the vegetables are tender and slightly charred around the edges.

VARIATIONS

• This is a very easy, pretty dish and you can vary the choice of vegetables according to what is in the market. Baby vegetables are excellent roasted. Tiny fennel, leeks and squash appear seasonally in supermarkets. Judge the roasting time by their volume.

• Aubergines (eggplants) are frequently included in this mixture, and their flavour is delicious, but they turn a slightly unappetizing grey colour when cooked and served plain.

RICE AND PASTA

Paella — that glorious combination of saffron rice, with shellfish, chicken or rabbit — is probably the dish most commonly associated with Spain. But there are many more classic festival and family dishes that combine rice with vegetables and even bananas. Pasta is a 500~year~old tradition, and comes in the same versatile combinations as the rice.

CUBAN-STYLE RICE

ARROZ A LA CUBANA, GARNISHED WITH FRIED EGGS AND BANANAS, IS POPULAR IN THE CANARY ISLANDS AND CATALONIA. IT MAKES AN EASY AND SUBSTANTIAL SUPPER DISH. BACON IS SOMETIMES ADDED TO THE TOMATO SAUCE, OR IS FRIED AND SERVED WITH THE EGGS.

SERVES FOUR

INGREDIENTS
    3 garlic cloves
    120ml/4fl oz/½ cup olive oil
    300g/11oz/1½ cups long
      grain rice
    15g/½oz/1 tbsp butter
    4 small bananas or 2 large bananas
    4 large (US extra large) eggs
    salt and paprika
For the tomato sauce
    30ml/2 tbsp olive oil
    1 onion, chopped
    2 garlic cloves, finely chopped
    800g/1lb 12oz can tomatoes
    4 thyme or oregano sprigs
    ground black pepper

1 Make the tomato sauce. Heat the oil in a pan, add the onion and garlic and fry gently, stirring, until soft. Stir in the tomatoes and thyme or oregano sprigs and simmer gently for 5 minutes. Add seasoning to taste. Remove the herb sprigs and keep the sauce warm.

2 Put 850ml/1 pint 8fl oz/3½ cups water in a pan with two whole garlic cloves and 15ml/1 tbsp oil. Bring to the boil, add the rice and cook for 18 minutes until it is done, and the liquid has been absorbed.

3 Heat a pan with 30ml/2 tbsp oil and gently fry one chopped garlic clove. Tip in the rice, stir, season well, then turn off the heat and cover the pan.

4 Heat the butter in a frying pan with 15ml/1 tbsp oil. Halve the bananas lengthways and fry briefly on both sides. Keep them warm.

5 Add 60ml/4 tbsp oil to the pan and fry the eggs over a medium-high heat, so that the edges turn golden. Season with salt and paprika. Serve the rice surrounded by tomato sauce and garnish with bananas and fried eggs.

ALICANTE CRUSTED RICE

PAELLA CON COSTRA IS AN UNUSUAL PAELLA WITH AN EGG CRUST THAT IS FINISHED IN THE OVEN.
THE CRUST SEALS IN ALL THE AROMAS UNTIL IT IS BROKEN OPEN AT THE TABLE.

SERVES SIX

INGREDIENTS
  45ml/3 tbsp olive oil
  200g/7oz *butifarra*, fresh sausages
    or frying chorizo, sliced
  2 tomatoes, peeled, seeded
    and chopped
  175g/6oz lean cubed pork
  175g/6oz skinless, boneless chicken
    breast or rabbit, cut into chunks
  350g/12oz/1¾ cups paella rice
  900ml–1 litre/1½–1¾ pints/
    3¾–4 cups hot chicken stock
  pinch of saffron threads (0.2g)
  150g/5oz/⅔ cup cooked chickpeas
  6 large (US extra large) eggs
  salt and ground black pepper

1 Preheat the oven to 190°C/375°F/
Gas 5. Heat the oil in a flameproof
casserole and fry the sausage until
browned. Add the tomatoes and fry until
reduced. Stir in the pork and chicken or
rabbit pieces and cook for 2–3 minutes
until the meat has browned lightly, stirring.

2 Add the rice to the pan, stir over the
heat for about 1 minute, then pour in
the hot stock. Add the saffron, season
to taste, and stir well.

3 Bring to the boil, then lower the heat
and add the chickpeas. Cover the
casserole tightly with the lid and cook
over a low heat for about 20 minutes or
until the rice is tender.

4 Beat the eggs with a little water and a
pinch of salt and pour over the rice.
Place the casserole, uncovered, in the
oven and cook for about 10 minutes,
until the eggs have set and browned
slightly on top. Serve the paella straight
from the casserole.

PAELLA VALENCIANA

A WORLD FAMOUS MIXTURE OF THE FINEST SPANISH INGREDIENTS, VALENCIA'S PAELLA CONTAINS CHICKEN, SHELLFISH AND VEGETABLES IN SUCCULENT SAFFRON RICE. IT HAS BECOME A CELEBRATION DISH THROUGHOUT SPAIN, AND SPAIN'S BEST-KNOWN DISH ABROAD. TO DRINK, CHOOSE A RED VALDEPEÑAS, WHICH WILL GO WELL WITH THE ROBUST FLAVOURS OF THE PAELLA.

SERVES SIX TO EIGHT

INGREDIENTS

90ml/6 tbsp white wine
450g/1lb fresh mussels, scrubbed
115g/4oz/scant 1 cup small
  shelled broad (fava) beans
150g/5oz green beans, cut into
  short lengths
90ml/6 tbsp olive oil
6 small skinless, boneless
  chicken breast portions, cut
  into large pieces
150g/5oz pork fillet, cubed
6–8 large raw prawn (shrimp) tails,
  deveined, or 12 smaller raw prawns
2 onions, chopped
2–3 garlic cloves, finely chopped
1 red (bell) pepper, seeded
  and sliced
2 ripe tomatoes, peeled, seeded
  and chopped
60ml/4 tbsp chopped fresh parsley
900ml/1½ pints/3¾ cups
  chicken stock
pinch of saffron threads (0.25g),
  soaked in 30ml/2 tbsp hot water
350g/12oz/1¾ cups paella rice,
  washed and drained
225g/8oz frying chorizo, sliced
115g/4oz/1 cup peas
6–8 stuffed green olives, sliced
salt, paprika and black pepper

COOK'S TIP
Paella is a very easy dish to make with the right pan and, more importantly, the right heat. Traditionally it is cooked outdoors on a wide bed of hot charcoal. Indoors a big heat source such as a large hot plate is needed.

Without this steady heat, the pan needs to be moved constantly, or the rice cooks in the centre, but not round the outside. Overcome this problem by cooking it in a hot oven.

1 Heat the wine and add the mussels, discarding any that do not close when tapped. Cover and steam until opened. Reserve the liquid and mussels separately, discarding any that do not open.

2 Briefly cook the broad beans and green beans in boiling water, then drain. Pop the broad beans out of their skins.

3 Heat 45ml/3 tbsp oil in a large paella pan or wide flameproof casserole. Season the chicken with salt and paprika, and put in, skin downwards. Fry, turning until browned on all sides. Reserve on a plate. Season the pork with salt and paprika. Add 15ml/1 tbsp oil and fry the seasoned pork until browned evenly. Reserve with the chicken. Fry the prawns briefly in the same pan, but reserve them separately.

4 Heat the remaining oil and fry the onions and garlic for 3–4 minutes until golden brown. Add the red pepper, cook for 2–3 minutes, then stir in the chopped tomatoes and parsley and cook until thick.

5 If cooking in the oven (see Cook's Tip) preheat to 190°C/375°F/Gas 5. Stir the chicken stock, the reserved mussel liquid and the saffron liquid into the vegetables. Season well with salt and pepper and bring the mixture to the boil. When the liquid is bubbling, throw in all the rice. Stir once, then add the chicken pieces, pork, shellfish, beans, chorizo and peas.

6 Transfer the pan to the oven and cook for 15–18 minutes until the rice is done. Alternatively, cook over medium-high heat for about 10 minutes. Then lower the heat and start to move the pan. A big pan needs to shift every 2–3 minutes, moving the edge of the pan round over the heat, then back to the centre. Cook until the rice is done – another 10–12 minutes.

7 Arrange the mussels and olives on top. Cover with a lid (or damp dishtowel) and leave to stand for 10 minutes, until all the liquid is absorbed. Serve straight from the pan.

COOK'S TIP
Spain exports saffron in little boxes labelled with the weight. A 0.3g packet contains 50–60 threads, enough to flavour three small dishes. A dish such as paella needs two-thirds – measured by eye. The amount of rice used in this recipe could take the whole 0.3g – and in Spain it probably would – so enjoy.

SEAFOOD PAELLA

THIS IS A GREAT DISH TO SERVE TO GUESTS ON A SPECIAL OCCASION. A SEAFOOD PAELLA ALWAYS LOOKS SPECTACULAR AND A BED OF SCENTED RICE IS THE PERFECT WAY TO DISPLAY A SELECTION OF MARISCOS (SEAFOOD). THIS PARTICULAR PAELLA CONTAINS A MAGNIFICENT COMBINATION OF SQUID, PRAWNS, MUSSELS AND CLAMS AS WELL AS SPICY CHORIZO AND SUCCULENT VEGETABLES.

SERVES FOUR

INGREDIENTS

45ml/3 tbsp olive oil
1 Spanish (Bermuda) onion, chopped
2 large garlic cloves, chopped
150g/5oz frying chorizo, sliced
300g/11oz small squid, cleaned
1 red (bell) pepper, cut into strips
4 tomatoes, peeled, seeded and
  diced or 200g/7oz can tomatoes
500ml/17fl oz/2¼ cups chicken
  stock, plus a little extra
105ml/7 tbsp dry white wine
200g/7oz/1 cup paella rice
pinch of saffron threads (0.2g),
  crumbled
150g/5oz/generous 1 cup peas
12 large cooked prawns (shrimp),
  in the shell or 8 peeled scampi
  (extra large shrimp)
450g/1lb fresh mussels, scrubbed
450g/1lb clams, scrubbed
4 cooked king prawns (jumbo shrimp)
  or scampi, in the shells
salt and ground black pepper
chopped fresh parsley and lemon
  wedges, to garnish

1 Heat the olive oil in a paella pan or large frying pan, add the onion and garlic and fry until translucent. Add the chorizo and fry until lightly golden.

2 If the squid are very small, leave them whole, otherwise cut the bodies into rings and the tentacles into pieces. Add the squid to the pan and sauté over a high heat for 2 minutes.

3 Stir in the pepper and tomatoes and simmer gently for 5 minutes, until the pepper is tender. Pour in the stock and wine, stir well and bring to the boil. Stir in the rice and saffron and season well. Spread the contents evenly over the base of the pan. Bring the liquid back to the boil, then lower the heat and simmer for about 10 minutes.

4 Gently stir the peas, prawns or scampi, mussels and clams into the rice, then cook for a further 15–20 minutes, until the rice is tender and all the mussels and clams have opened. (Discard any that remain closed.) If the paella seems dry, stir in a little more hot stock.

5 Remove the pan from the heat and arrange the king prawns or scampi on top. Cover and leave to stand for 5 minutes. Sprinkle the paella with chopped parsley and serve from the pan, accompanied by lemon wedges.

VEGETABLE RICE POT

IN THIS ARROZ DE VERDURAS, *FRESH SEASONAL VEGETABLES ARE COOKED IN SLIGHTLY SPICED RICE. ALWAYS TASTE STOCK BEFORE ADDING IT TO RICE: THIS IS YOUR CHANCE TO REDUCE AND CONCENTRATE IT, OR TO ADD WINE, A BIT OF A STOCK CUBE, OR EVEN SOY SAUCE FOR EXTRA FLAVOUR. IF THE STOCK LACKS TASTE, SO WILL THE FINAL DISH.*

SERVES FOUR

INGREDIENTS

1 large aubergine (eggplant)
45ml/3 tbsp olive oil
2 onions, quartered and sliced
2 garlic cloves, finely chopped
1 red (bell) pepper, halved, seeded and sliced
1 yellow (bell) pepper, halved, seeded and sliced
200g/7oz fine green beans, halved
115g/4oz/1½ cups brown cap (cremini) mushrooms, halved
300g/11oz/1½ cups paella rice, washed and drained
1 dried chilli, seeded and crumbled
1 litre/1¾ pints/4 cups chicken stock
115g/4oz/1 cup peas
60ml/4 tbsp chopped fresh parsley
salt and ground black pepper
fresh parsley or coriander (cilantro) leaves, to garnish

1 Halve the aubergine lengthways, then cut it into slices. Spread them out in a large colander or on a draining board, sprinkle with salt and leave for about 30 minutes to drain, then rinse under cold running water and pat dry with kitchen paper.

2 Heat 30ml/2 tbsp olive oil in a wide flameproof casserole or sauté pan over a high heat. Add the aubergine slices and sauté until slightly golden, stirring occasionally, then transfer to kitchen paper to drain.

3 Add the remaining oil to the pan and cook the onion and garlic until soft. Add the peppers, green beans and mushrooms and cook briefly.

4 Add the drained rice and stir for 1–2 minutes, then add the aubergine and stir. Add the chilli and seasoning. Taste the stock and pour in. Add the peas and parsley and mix together.

5 Bring to boiling point, cover and cook over a low heat, for 20–25 minutes, checking the liquid level towards the end (the rice should absorb the liquid, but not burn). When the rice is tender, turn off the heat, cover the pan and leave to stand for 10 minutes for the remaining liquid to be absorbed. Garnish with parsley or coriander and serve.

VARIATIONS
• Almost any roughly chopped or sliced vegetables can be used in this dish. Broccoli, carrots, cauliflower, courgettes (zucchini) and okra are all suitable – or try using frozen corn in place of all or some of the peas.
• To make a tomato-flavoured rice, use a 400g/14oz can chopped tomatoes in place of 350ml/12fl oz/1½ cups of the chicken stock.

CALDERETE OF RICE WITH ALLIOLI

COOKING RICE IN FISH STOCK GIVES IT SUCH A SPLENDID FLAVOUR THAT IT IS OFTEN EATEN ON ITS OWN — ARROZ ABANDA — SERVED IN A LITTLE CAULDRON AND ACCOMPANIED BY ALLIOLI. THE FISH THEN FOLLOWS AS A SEPARATE COURSE. IF YOU PREFER, THE FISH CAN BE RETURNED TO THE CASSEROLE WHILE THE DISH IS STILL LIQUID, AND THE FISH AND RICE EATEN WITH THE SAUCE.

SERVES SIX

INGREDIENTS

    1.6kg/3½lb mixed fish on the
      bone, such as snapper, bream,
      grey or red mullet, or bass
    45ml/3 tbsp olive oil
    6 garlic cloves, smashed
    1 *ñora* chilli or 1 hot dried chilli,
      seeded and chopped
    250g/9oz ripe tomatoes, peeled,
      seeded and chopped
    pinch of saffron threads (0.25g)
    30ml/2 tbsp dry Martini or
      white wine
    1 tomato, finely diced
    30ml/2 tbsp chopped
      fresh parsley
    400g/14oz/2 cups paella
      rice, washed
    115g/4oz tiny unshelled shrimps
    salt and ground black pepper
For the stock
    1 onion, chopped
    2 garlic cloves, chopped
    1 celery stick, chopped
    1 carrot, chopped
    1 litre/1¾ pints/4 cups water
For the allioli
    4 garlic cloves, finely chopped
    2.5ml/½ tsp salt
    5ml/1 tsp lemon juice
    2 egg yolks
    250ml/8fl oz/1 cup olive oil

1 Remove the heads from the fish. Working from the head end, cut the skin along the top of the back and work the fillets off the bone. Trim as needed, put the fillets on a plate, salt them lightly, cover and place in the refrigerator until required.

2 Make the fish stock. Put the bones, heads, tails and any other remaining bits into a large pan with the onion, garlic, celery, carrot and water. Bring to the boil, then reduce the heat, cover with a lid and simmer gently for about 30 minutes.

3 Make the allioli. Put the chopped garlic in a large mortar (or small blender) with the salt and lemon juice and reduce to a purée. Add the egg yolks and mix thoroughly. Gradually work in the oil (drop by drop at first if using a mortar) to make a thick, mayonnaise-like sauce.

4 Put 15ml/1 tbsp of the olive oil in a small pan and add the whole smashed garlic cloves and dried chilli pieces. Fry for a few minutes until the garlic looks roasted. Add the chopped tomato halfway through, crumble in the saffron and cook to form a sauce. Pour the sauce into a small blender and purée until smooth.

5 Heat the remaining 30ml/2 tbsp oil in a large pan or a wide flameproof casserole and fry the fish pieces until they begin to stiffen. Strain the fish stock into a jug (pitcher), then add 900ml/1½ pints/3¾ cups stock and the tomato sauce to the fish. Cook the fish gently for a further 3–4 minutes, until slightly underdone.

6 Remove the fish pieces from the pan with a slotted spoon to a serving dish. Season lightly, sprinkle with the Martini or wine, diced tomato and parsley. Cover with foil and keep warm.

7 Add the rice to the stock, stir, season and bring to a simmer. Cook for 18–20 minutes. Before all the liquid is absorbed, stir in the shrimps. When the rice is tender, cover and turn off the heat. Stand until all the liquid is absorbed: about 5 minutes. Serve from the pan, accompanied by the allioli.

8 When the rice course is almost finished, uncover the fish. Stir the fish juices into the remains of the allioli, then pour over the fish. Eat on the same plates as the rice.

SIMPLE RICE SALAD

IN THIS QUICK AND EASY SIDE DISH, RICE AND A SELECTION OF CHOPPED SALAD VEGETABLES ARE
SERVED IN A WELL-FLAVOURED DRESSING TO MAKE A PRETTY SALAD.

SERVES SIX

INGREDIENTS
  275g/10oz/1½ cups long grain rice
  1 bunch spring onions (scallions),
    finely sliced
  1 green (bell) pepper, seeded and
    finely diced
  1 yellow (bell) pepper, seeded and
    finely diced
  225g/8oz tomatoes, peeled, seeded
    and chopped
  30ml/2 tbsp chopped fresh flat leaf
    parsley or coriander (cilantro)
For the dressing
  75ml/5 tbsp mixed olive oil and extra
    virgin olive oil
  15ml/1 tbsp sherry vinegar
  5ml/1 tsp strong Dijon mustard
  salt and ground black pepper

1 Cook the rice in a large pan of lightly salted boiling water for 10–12 minutes, until tender but still *al dente*. Be careful not to overcook it.

2 Drain the rice well in a sieve (strainer), rinse thoroughly under cold running water and drain again. Leave the rice to cool completely.

3 Place the rice in a large serving bowl. Add the spring onions, peppers, tomatoes and parsley or coriander.

4 Make the dressing. Place all the ingredients in a screw-top jar, put the lid on and shake vigorously until well mixed. Stir the dressing into the rice and check the seasoning.

MOORS AND CHRISTIANS

MOROS Y CRISTIANOS IS MADE EVERY YEAR IN VALENCIA AT THE FESTIVAL CELEBRATING AN ANCIENT VICTORY OF THE CHRISTIANS OVER THE MOORS. THE BLACK BEANS REPRESENT THE LATTER, AND THE WHITE RICE THE FORMER. THIS IS AN ELEGANT MODERN VERSION OF A TRADITIONAL DISH.

SERVES SIX

INGREDIENTS
  400g/14oz/2 cups black beans,
    soaked overnight
  1 onion, quartered
  1 carrot, sliced
  1 celery stick, sliced
  1 garlic clove, finely chopped
  1 bay leaf
  5ml/1 tsp paprika
  45ml/3 tbsp olive oil
  juice of 1 orange
  300g/11oz/1½ cups long grain rice
  salt and cayenne pepper
For the garnish
  chopped fresh parsley
  thin wedges of orange
  sliced red onion

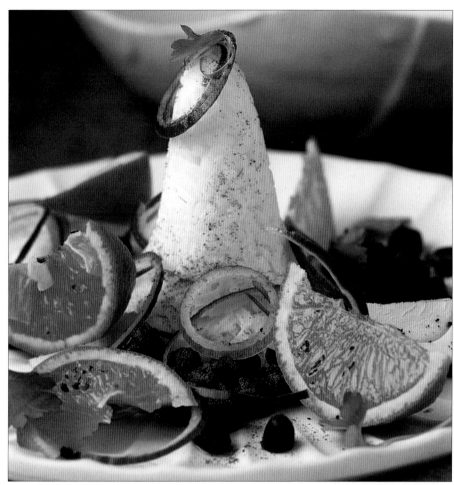

1 Put the beans in a large pan with the onion, carrot, celery, garlic and bay leaf and 1.75 litres/3 pints/7½ cups water. Bring to the boil and cook rapidly for 10 minutes, then reduce the heat and simmer for 1 hour, topping up the water if necessary. When the beans are almost tender, drain, discarding the vegetables. Return the beans to a clean pan.

2 Blend the paprika and oil with cayenne pepper to taste and stir into the beans with the orange juice. Top up with a little water, if necessary. Heat gently until barely simmering, then cover and cook for 10–15 minutes until the beans are completely tender. Remove from the heat and allow to stand in the liquid for 15 minutes. Season with salt to taste.

3 Meanwhile, cook the rice in boiling water until tender. Drain, then pack into a buttered bowl or individual moulds and allow to stand for 10 minutes.

4 Unmould the rice on to a serving plate and arrange the black beans around the edge. Garnish with parsley, orange wedges and red onion slices.

FIDEOS CON ALMEJAS

*PASTA THE EAST COAST WAY, FIDEOS ARE LENGTHS OF SPAGHETTI, SHORTER THAN A FINGER. THIS
SENSATIONAL DISH IS RATHER LIKE PAELLA MADE WITH PASTA — JUST AS NICE, AND A GREAT DEAL
EASIER. IT IS POPULAR ALONG THE MEDITERRANEAN COAST — THE LEVANTE AND THE SOUTH AROUND
MÁLAGA. THE MILKY FLESH OF CLAMS CONTRASTS WONDERFULLY WITH THE FIRMER PASTA AND FENNEL.*

SERVES FOUR TO SIX

INGREDIENTS

  30ml/2 tbsp olive oil
  1 large Spanish (Bermuda) onion,
    chopped
  1 garlic clove, finely chopped
  2 large ripe tomatoes
  750ml/1¼ pint/3 cups fish stock
  1kg/2¼lb clams, cleaned
  120ml/4fl oz/½ cup anis spirit, such
    as Ricard or Pernod
  120ml/4fl oz/½ cup dry white wine,
    such as Torres Viña Sol
  juice of ¼ lemon
  300g/11oz spaghetti, broken into
    5cm/2in lengths
  1 fennel bulb, sliced in thin strips
  30ml/2 tbsp chopped fresh parsley
  salt and ground pepper
  fennel fronds or fresh dill, to garnish

1 Heat the oil in a casserole big enough
to contain all the ingredients. Fry the
onion gently until soft. Add the garlic.

2 Put the tomatoes in a bowl and pour
over boiling water. After 10 minutes, peel
the tomatoes on a plate and discard
the seeds. Chop the flesh, add to the
casserole and strain the tomato juices into
the pan. Cook until reduced to a pulp,
then add 250ml/8fl oz/1 cup of the stock.

3 Discard any open or cracked clams.
Add the rest to the pan in three
batches. As they open, remove most
from the shells and transfer to a plate.
Discard any clams that remain shut.

4 Add the anis spirit and white wine to
the sauce, plus the remaining fish
stock and lemon juice, to taste. Add
the pasta and sliced fennel. Season
and simmer, partially covered, for
10 minutes. Stir every now and then
to separate the strands, and to make
sure the pasta is not sticking.

5 When the pasta is cooked, stir in the
parsley and check the seasoning. Tip
the clams across the top and cover
tightly. Leave to stand for 10 minutes,
so the clams warm through and all the
liquid is absorbed. Serve in bowls,
sprinkled with the fennel fronds or dill.

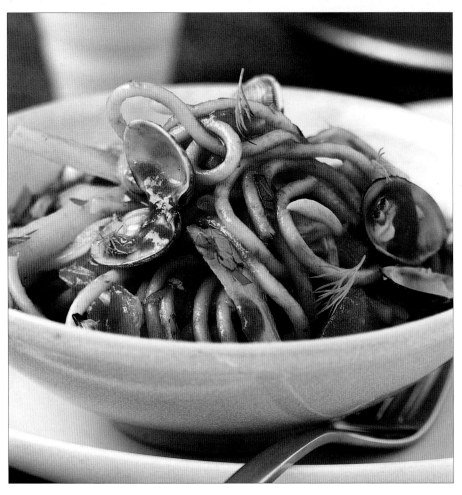

SAN ESTEBAN CANELONES

CATALANS ARE FOND OF PASTA, AND CANELONES ARE TRADITIONAL ON SAN ESTEBAN, THE DAY AFTER CHRISTMAS DAY, AND ARE OFTEN MADE IN LARGE QUANTITIES. TRY TO KEEP ALL THE CHOPPED STUFFING INGREDIENTS THE SAME SIZE — SMALL DICE. SPANISH STORES SELL SQUARES OF PASTA FOR COOKING THEN ROLLING, BUT READY PREPARED CANNELLONI TUBES HAVE BEEN USED HERE.

SERVES FOUR TO EIGHT

INGREDIENTS
    60ml/4 tbsp olive oil
    1 onion, finely chopped
    1 carrot, finely chopped
    2 garlic cloves, finely chopped
    2 ripe tomatoes, peeled and
        finely chopped
    2.5ml/½ tsp dried thyme
    150g/5oz raw chicken livers
        or cooked stuffing
    150g/5oz raw pork or cooked ham,
        gammon or sausage
    250g/9oz raw or cooked chicken
    25g/1oz/2 tbsp butter
    5ml/1 tsp fresh thyme
    30ml/2 tbsp brandy
    90ml/6 tbsp crème fraîche or
        double (heavy) cream
    16 no pre-cook cannelloni tubes
    75g/3oz/1 cup grated fresh
        Parmesan cheese
    salt and ground black pepper
    green salad, to serve
For the white sauce
    50g/2oz/¼ cup butter
    50g/2oz/½ cup plain
        (all-purpose) flour
    900ml/1½ pints/3¾ cups milk
    fresh nutmeg, to taste

1 Heat the oil in a large frying pan, add the onion, carrot, garlic and tomatoes and cook over a low heat, stirring, for about 10 minutes or until very soft. Meanwhile, chop all the meats to the same size, keeping the fresh and cooked meat apart.

2 Add the butter, then the raw meat, to the centre of the frying pan and cook until coloured. Then add the remaining meats and sprinkle first with thyme, then with the brandy. Stir, then warm through and reduce the liquid.

3 Pour in the crème fraîche or cream, season to taste and leave to simmer for about 10 minutes. Allow to cool briefly.

4 Preheat the oven to 190°C/375°F/ Gas 5. Make the white sauce. Melt the butter in a small pan, add the flour and cook, stirring, for 1–2 minutes. Gradually stir in the milk, a little at a time. Bring to simmering point, stirring until the sauce is smooth. Grate in nutmeg to taste, then season with plenty of salt and black pepper.

5 Spoon a little of the white sauce into a baking dish. Fill the cannelloni tubes with the meat mixture and arrange in a single layer in the dish. Pour the remaining white sauce over them, then sprinkle with the Parmesan cheese. Bake for 35–40 minutes, or until the pasta is tender. Leave for 10 minutes before serving with green salad.

ANDRAJOS

This is a rich dish of hare, wine and mushrooms, flavoured with herbs and pine nuts. The name means "rags and tatters"; it was a shepherds' dish and the shepherd would have made his own simple flour and water pasta, cut into squares. Dried pasta squares are still sold in Spain to make cannelloni. This recipe uses bought lasagne, which needs to be broken up. The sauce permeates the pasta and transforms the chicken.

SERVES SIX

INGREDIENTS

- 800g/1¾lb hare meat and bone (the front legs and rib end)
- 200ml/7fl oz/scant 1 cup red wine
- 120–150ml/4–5fl oz/½–⅔ cup olive oil
- 150g/5oz smoked bacon lardons, or diced pancetta
- 2 onions, chopped
- 2 fat garlic cloves, finely chopped
- 8 baby onions, peeled
- 4 carrots, diced
- 4 chicken thighs, halved along the bone and seasoned
- seasoned plain (all-purpose) flour, for dusting
- 350g/12oz small open cap mushrooms
- 600ml/1 pint/2½ cups stock
- 5ml/1 tsp dried thyme
- 1 bay leaf
- 250g/9oz dried lasagne sheets
- 90ml/6 tbsp chopped parsley
- 30ml/2 tbsp pine nuts
- salt and ground black pepper

1 Starting at least two days ahead, cut the hare into portions and put in a bowl. Pour over the red wine and 15ml/ 1 tbsp of the oil and leave to marinate in the refrigerator for at least 24 hours.

COOK'S TIP
This dish uses the front part of the hare, while the back legs and saddle are best kept for a grander dish.

2 Heat 30ml/2 tbsp olive oil in a flameproof casserole, add the bacon or pancetta, chopped onion and garlic and fry until the onion is translucent. Halfway through add the whole baby onions and diced carrots, and continue cooking, stirring occasionally.

3 Heat 45ml/3 tbsp oil in a large frying pan and fry the seasoned chicken pieces on both sides until golden brown. Transfer to the casserole.

4 Remove the hare from the red wine marinade, reserving the liquid. Blot the meat well on kitchen paper and dredge with the seasoned flour until well coated. Add more oil to the frying pan, if necessary, and fry the meat on all sides until browned.

5 Meanwhile, reserve eight of the smallest open cap mushrooms. Quarter the remaining mushrooms and add to the casserole. Continue cooking the hare in the frying pan, stirring every now and then, until browned.

6 When the hare is ready, arrange the pieces in the casserole. Pour the reserved marinade into the frying pan to deglaze it, then pour the juices into the casserole. Add the stock, dried thyme and bay leaf and season with salt and pepper. Cook over a low heat for 1½ hours, until the meat is tender. Leave to cool completely.

7 When ready to serve, bring plenty of water to the boil in a large roasting pan with 5ml/1 tsp salt and 15ml/1 tbsp oil. Break up the lasagne sheets and spread out the pieces in the pan. Cook for 7–8 minutes until soft, moving the pieces around to prevent them from sticking.

8 Remove all the meat from the bones and return to the casserole with 60ml/ 4 tbsp of the parsley. Bring to a simmer. Stir the drained pasta into the sauce. Heat 15ml/1 tbsp oil in a small pan and fry the reserved mushrooms, then arrange them on top. Sprinkle with the remaining parsley and the pine nuts, and serve.

FISH AND SHELLFISH

With its long coastline, Spain has some of the best fishing in the world and seafood is one of the glories of Spanish cooking. There are delicious appetizers, colourful salads and delightful but simple combinations with lemon, tomatoes or potatoes, and hearty stews such as Zarzuela make a delicious main course.

SARDINES EN ESCABECHE

THE ARABS INVENTED MARINADES AS A MEANS OF PRESERVING POULTRY, MEAT AND GAME, AND ESCABECHE MEANS "ACID" IN ARABIC. IN SPAIN THIS METHOD WAS ENTHUSIASTICALLY ADOPTED AS A MEANS OF KEEPING FISH FRESH. THE FISH ARE ALWAYS FRIED FIRST AND THEN STORED IN VINEGAR.

3 Heat the olive oil in a frying pan and fry the sardines for 2–3 minutes on each side. With a metal spatula, remove the fish from the pan to a plate and allow to cool, then pack them in a single layer in a large shallow dish.

4 To make the marinade, add the olive oil to the oil remaining in the frying pan. Fry the onion and garlic gently for 5–10 minutes until soft and translucent, stirring occasionally. Add the bay leaves, cloves, chilli and paprika, with pepper to taste. Fry, stirring frequently, for another 1–2 minutes.

SERVES TWO TO FOUR

INGREDIENTS
  12–16 sardines, cleaned
  seasoned plain (all-purpose) flour,
    for dusting
  30ml/2 tbsp olive oil
  roasted red onion, green (bell) pepper
    and tomatoes, to garnish
For the marinade
  90ml/6 tbsp olive oil
  1 onion, sliced
  1 garlic clove, crushed
  3–4 bay leaves
  2 cloves
  1 dried red chilli, seeded
    and chopped
  5ml/1 tsp paprika
  120ml/4fl oz/½ cup wine
    or sherry vinegar
  120ml/4fl oz/½ cup white wine
  salt and ground black pepper

1 Using a sharp knife, cut the heads off the sardines and split each of them along the belly. Turn the fish over so that the backbone is uppermost. Press down along the backbone to loosen it, then carefully lift out the backbone and as many of the remaining little bones as possible.

2 Close the sardines up again and dust them with seasoned flour.

5 Stir in the vinegar, wine and a little salt. Allow to bubble up, then pour over the sardines. The marinade should cover the fish completely. When the fish is cool, cover and chill overnight or for up to three days. Serve the sardines and their marinade, garnished with the onion, pepper and tomatoes.

VARIATION
Other oily fish such as herrings or sprats (small whitebait) are very good prepared in this way. White fish can also be used.

SKATE WITH BITTER SALAD LEAVES

THIS DISH IS POPULAR IN GALICIA, WHICH IS FAMOUS FOR BOTH ITS SKATE AND ITS WATERCRESS. SKATE HAS A DELICIOUS SWEET FLAVOUR, ENHANCED HERE BY ORANGE. IT CONTRASTS WELL WITH ANY BITTER LEAVES — BUY A BAG OF MIXED SALAD LEAVES FOR CONTRASTING TEXTURES AND FLAVOURS.

SERVES FOUR

INGREDIENTS
    800g/1¾lb skate wings
    15ml/1 tbsp white wine vinegar
    4 black peppercorns
    1 fresh thyme sprig
    175g/6oz bitter salad leaves,
      such as frisée, rocket (arugula),
      radicchio, escarole, lamb's lettuce
      (mâche) and watercress
    1 orange
    2 tomatoes, peeled, seeded
      and diced
For the dressing
    15ml/1 tbsp white wine vinegar
    45ml/3 tbsp extra virgin olive oil
    1 bunch spring onions (scallions),
      whites finely chopped
    salt, paprika and black pepper
    crusty bread, to serve

1 Put the skate wings into a large shallow pan, cover with cold water and add the vinegar, peppercorns and thyme. Bring to the boil, then poach gently for 8–10 minutes, until the flesh comes away easily from the bones.

2 Make the dressing. Whisk together the vinegar, oil and spring onions and season with salt, paprika and pepper.

3 Put the salad leaves in a large bowl, pour over the dressing and toss well. Remove the rind from the orange using a zester, then peel it, removing all the pith. Slice into thin rounds.

4 Flake the fish, discarding the bones, and add to the salad. Add a pinch of zest, the orange slices and tomatoes, toss gently and serve with bread.

BAKED TROUT <u>WITH</u> RICE, TOMATOES <u>AND</u> NUTS

TROUT IS VERY POPULAR IN SPAIN, PARTICULARLY IN THE NORTH, WHERE IT IS FISHED IN MANY RIVERS. HERE IS A MODERN RECIPE FOR TRUCHA RELLENA, BAKED IN FOIL WITH A RICE STUFFING IN WHICH SUN-DRIED TOMATOES HAVE BEEN USED IN PLACE OF THE MORE TRADITIONAL CHILLIES.

SERVES FOUR

INGREDIENTS

2 fresh trout, about 500g/1¼lb each
75g/3oz/¾ cup mixed unsalted
   almonds, pine nuts or hazelnuts
25ml/1½ tbsp olive oil, plus extra
   for drizzling
1 small onion, finely chopped
10ml/2 tsp grated fresh root ginger
175g/6oz/1½ cups cooked white
   long grain rice
4 tomatoes, peeled and very
   finely chopped
4 sun-dried tomatoes in oil, drained
   and chopped
30ml/2 tbsp chopped fresh tarragon
2 fresh tarragon sprigs
salt and ground black pepper
dressed green salad leaves,
   to serve

1 Preheat the oven to 190°C/375°F/ Gas 5. If the trout is unfilleted, use a sharp knife to fillet it. Remove any tiny bones remaining in the cavity using a pair of tweezers.

2 Spread out the nuts in a shallow tin (pan) and bake for 3–4 minutes until golden brown, shaking the tin occasionally. Chop the nuts roughly.

3 Heat the olive oil in a small frying pan and fry the onion for 3–4 minutes until soft and translucent. Stir in the grated ginger, cook for a further 1 minute, then spoon into a mixing bowl.

4 Stir the rice, chopped tomatoes, sun-dried tomatoes, toasted nuts and tarragon into the onion mixture. Season the stuffing well.

5 Place the trout on individual large pieces of oiled foil and spoon the stuffing into the cavities. Add a sprig of tarragon and a drizzle of olive oil or oil from the sun-dried tomatoes.

6 Fold the foil over to enclose each trout completely, and put the parcels in a large roasting pan. Bake for about 20 minutes or until the fish is just tender. Cut the fish into thick slices. Serve with the salad leaves.

COOK'S TIP

You will need about 75g/3oz/³/4 cup of uncooked rice to produce 175g/6oz/ 1¹/2 cups cooked rice.

TRUCHAS A LA NAVARRA

TRADITIONALLY, THE TROUT WOULD HAVE COME FROM MOUNTAIN STREAMS AND BEEN STUFFED AND WRAPPED IN LOCALLY CURED HAM. ONE OF THE BEAUTIES OF THIS METHOD IS THAT THE SKINS COME OFF IN ONE PIECE, LEAVING THE SUCCULENT, MOIST FLESH TO BE EATEN WITH THE CRISPED, SALT HAM.

SERVES FOUR

INGREDIENTS

4 brown or rainbow trout, about
   250g/9oz each, cleaned
16 thin slices Serrano ham, about
   200g/7oz
50g/2oz/¼ cup melted butter, plus
   extra for greasing
salt and ground black pepper
buttered potatoes, to
   serve (optional)

1 Extend the belly cavity of each trout, cutting up one side of the backbone. Slip a knife behind the rib bones to loosen them (sometimes just flexing the fish makes them pop up). Snip these off from both sides with scissors, and season the fish well inside.

2 Preheat the grill (broiler) to high, with a shelf in the top position. Line a baking tray with foil and butter it.

3 Working with the fish on the foil, fold a piece of ham into each belly. Use smaller or broken bits of ham for this, and reserve the eight best slices.

4 Brush each trout with a little butter, seasoning the outside lightly with salt and pepper. Wrap two ham slices round each one, crossways, tucking the ends into the belly. Grill (broil) the trout for 4 minutes, then carefully turn them over with a metal spatula, rolling them across on the belly, so the ham doesn't come loose, and grill for a further 4 minutes.

5 Serve the trout very hot, with any spare butter spooned over the top. Diners should open the trout on their plates, and eat them from the inside, pushing the flesh off the skin.

SEA BASS IN A SALT CRUST

BAKING FISH IN A CRUST OF SEA SALT ENHANCES THE FLAVOUR AND BRINGS OUT THE TASTE OF THE SEA. IT IS ALSO THE EASIEST WAY THERE IS TO COOK A WHOLE FISH. IN SPAIN THE GILT-HEAD BREAM IS THE FISH MOST OFTEN USED, BUT ANY FIRM FISH, SUCH AS GREY MULLET, STRIPED BASS AND PORGY, CAN BE COOKED THIS WAY. BREAK OPEN THE CRUST AT THE TABLE TO RELEASE THE GLORIOUS AROMA.

SERVES FOUR TO SIX

INGREDIENTS

   1 sea bass, about 1kg/2¼lb,
     gutted and scaled
   1 sprig each of fresh fennel,
     rosemary and thyme
   mixed peppercorns
   2kg/4½lb coarse sea salt
   seaweed or samphire, to garnish
     (optional)
   lemon slices, to serve

COOK'S TIP

In the Mediterranean, fish in salt are often baked whole and ungutted. But supermarkets elsewhere always sell them gutted, so use the opportunity to add flavourings inside.

1 Preheat the oven to 240°C/475°F/ Gas 9. Fill the cavity of the sea bass with the fennel, rosemary and thyme sprigs and grind over some of the mixed peppercorns.

2 Spread half the salt in a shallow baking tray and lay the sea bass on it.

3 Cover the fish all over with a 1cm/½in layer of salt, pressing it down firmly. Bake for 30 minutes, until the salt coagulates and is beginning to colour.

4 To serve, leave the fish on the baking tray and garnish with seaweed or samphire, if using. Bring the fish to the table in its salt crust. Use a sharp knife to break open the crust.

COOK'S TIP

Once baked, the salt sticks to the fish skin, and brings it off. Scrape back the layer of salt and lift out the top fillet in sections. Snip the backbone with scissors and lift out. Discard the herbs and remove the bottom fillet pieces. Add a lemon slice to each plate.

BACALAO IN SPICY TOMATO WITH POTATOES

SALT COD IS A POPULAR INGREDIENT IN SPAIN, NOT JUST A LENTEN NECESSITY. IT IS THE SALT THAT MAKES THE FISH SO CHARACTERFUL, SO DON'T OVERSOAK IT FOR THIS TRADITIONAL BASQUE RECIPE. LOOK OUT FOR A LOIN PIECE, WHICH HAS VERY LITTLE WASTE; IF YOU CAN'T FIND ONE, BUY A LARGER PIECE TO ENSURE YOU HAVE ENOUGH ONCE ANY VERY DRY BITS HAVE BEEN REMOVED.

SERVES FOUR

INGREDIENTS

- 400g/14oz salt cod loin, soaked in cold water for 24 hours
- 30ml/2 tbsp olive oil
- 1 large onion, chopped
- 2 garlic cloves, finely chopped
- 1½ green (bell) peppers, seeded and chopped
- 500g/1¼lb ripe tomatoes, peeled and chopped, or a 400g/14oz can tomatoes
- 15ml/1 tbsp tomato purée (paste)
- 15ml/1 tbsp clear honey
- 1.5ml/¼ tsp dried thyme
- 2.5ml/½ tsp cayenne pepper
- juice of ½ lemon (optional)
- 2 potatoes
- 45ml/3 tbsp stale breadcrumbs
- 30ml/2 tbsp finely chopped fresh parsley
- salt and ground black pepper

1 Drain the salt cod and place in a pan. Pour over water to cover generously and bring to the boil. Remove the pan from the heat as soon as the water boils, then set aside until cold.

2 Heat the oil in a medium pan. Fry the onion, and add the garlic after 5 minutes. Add the chopped peppers and tomatoes, and cook gently to form a sauce. Stir in the tomato purée, honey, dried thyme, cayenne, black pepper and a little salt. Taste for seasoning: a little lemon juice will make it tangier.

3 Halve the potatoes lengthways and cut them into slices just thicker than a coin. Drain the fish, reserving the cooking water.

4 Preheat the grill (broiler) to medium with a shelf 15cm/6in below it. Bring the reserved fish cooking water to the boil and cook the potatoes for about 8 minutes. Do not add extra salt.

5 Remove the skin and bones from the cod, and pull it into small natural flakes. Spoon one-third of the tomato sauce into a flameproof casserole, top with the potatoes, fish and remaining sauce. Combine the breadcrumbs and parsley and sprinkle over. Heat the dish through under a grill for 10 minutes.

CHARGRILLED SQUID

CALAMARES A LA PLANCHA ARE TRADITIONALLY COOKED ON THE HOT GRIDDLE THAT IS AN ESSENTIAL PART OF EVERY SPANISH KITCHEN. THE METHOD IS FAST AND SIMPLE AND REALLY BRINGS OUT THE FLAVOUR OF THE SQUID. THIS DISH IS AN IDEAL FIRST COURSE FOR FOUR PEOPLE, OR CAN BE SERVED ON A BED OF RICE AS A MAIN DISH FOR TWO.

3 Heat a ridged griddle pan until hot. Add the body of one of the squid and cook over a medium heat for 2–3 minutes, pressing the squid with a metal spatula to keep it flat. Repeat on the other side. Cook the other squid body in the same way.

4 Cut the squid bodies into diagonal strips. If serving with rice, arrange the squid strips criss-cross on top. Keep hot.

5 Add the chopped tentacles and chillies to the pan and toss over a medium heat for 2 minutes. Stir in the wine, then drizzle over the squid. Garnish with chopped parsley.

SERVES TWO TO FOUR

INGREDIENTS

2 whole cleaned squid, with tentacles, about 275g/10oz each
75ml/5 tbsp olive oil
30ml/2 tbsp sherry vinegar
2 fresh red chillies, finely chopped
60ml/4 tbsp dry white wine
salt and ground black pepper
hot cooked rice, to serve (optional)
15–30ml/1–2 tbsp chopped parsley, to garnish

1 Make a lengthways cut down the side of the body of each squid, then open it out flat. Score the flesh on both sides of the bodies in a criss-cross pattern with the tip of a sharp knife. Chop the tentacles into short lengths. Place all the squid pieces in a non-metallic dish.

2 Whisk together the oil and vinegar in a small bowl. Add salt and pepper to taste, pour over the squid and toss to mix. Cover and leave to marinate for about 1 hour.

HAKE AND CLAMS WITH SALSA VERDE

MERLUZA EN SALSA VERDE IS A FAVOURITE BASQUE WAY OF COOKING HAKE, WHICH IS ONE OF THE MOST POPULAR AND PLENTIFUL FISH IN SPAIN. AS THEY BAKE, THE CLAMS OPEN UP AND ADD THEIR DELICIOUS SEA JUICES TO THE GREEN WINE AND PARSLEY SAUCE.

SERVES FOUR

INGREDIENTS

4 hake steaks, about 2cm/¾in thick
50g/2oz/½ cup plain (all-purpose)
  flour, for dusting, plus 30ml/2 tbsp
60ml/4 tbsp olive oil
15ml/1 tbsp lemon juice
1 small onion, finely chopped
4 garlic cloves, finely chopped
150ml/¼ pint/⅔ cup fish stock
150ml/¼ pint/⅔ cup white wine
90ml/6 tbsp chopped fresh parsley
75g/3oz/¾ cup frozen petits pois
16 fresh clams, cleaned
salt and ground black pepper

COOK'S TIP
To make fish stock, put 450g/1lb fish bones, head and skin in a large pan with 1 sliced onion, 1 sliced carrot, ½ sliced celery stalk, 3–4 thick parsley stalks, snapped in places, 1 bay leaf, 10ml/ 2 tsp lemon juice or wine vinegar and 175ml/6fl oz/¾ cup dry white wine or vermouth. Bring to the boil, then reduce the heat and simmer for 30 minutes. Strain. If you can't buy fish bits, collect fish leftovers in the freezer: prawn (shrimp) heads, the spines from cooked fish, poaching water from a salmon, and mussel or clam stock from opening the shellfish. It is also worth buying a small whole fish to add to the stock.

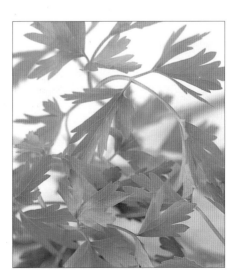

1 Preheat the oven to 180°C/350°F/ Gas 4. Season the fish, then dust with flour. Heat half the oil in a large pan, add the fish and fry for 1 minute on each side. Transfer to an ovenproof dish and sprinkle with the lemon juice.

2 Heat the remaining oil in a clean pan and fry the onion and garlic, stirring, until soft. Stir in the 30ml/2 tbsp flour and cook for about 1 minute.

3 Slowly add the stock and wine to the pan, stirring until thickened. Add 75ml/5 tbsp of the parsley and the petits pois to the sauce and season with plenty of salt and pepper.

4 Pour the sauce over the fish, and bake for 15–20 minutes, adding the clams 3–4 minutes before the end of the cooking time.

5 Discard any clams that do not open once cooked, then sprinkle the fish with with the remaining parsley and serve.

VARIATION
In Rioja country, on the banks of the River Ebro, this dish often includes fresh young asparagus tips as well as peas. Simply replace half the peas with asparagus tips.

OCTOPUS STEW

In Galicia, octopus stews are particularly popular and a common tapas dish is a simple stew with paprika, served on little wooden plates. Here the octopus is stewed with tomatoes and potatoes, to make a substantial main course. It is an ideal make-in-advance dish, because octopus can be tough, and benefits from long cooking to tenderize it.

SERVES FOUR TO SIX

INGREDIENTS
  1kg/2¼lb octopus, cleaned
  45ml/3 tbsp olive oil
  1 large red onion, chopped
  3 garlic cloves, finely chopped
  30ml/2 tbsp brandy
  300ml/½ pint/1¼ cups dry
    white wine
  800g/1¾lb ripe plum tomatoes,
    peeled and chopped or 2 × 400g/
    14oz cans chopped tomatoes
  1 dried red chilli, seeded
    and chopped
  1.5ml/¼ tsp paprika
  450g/1lb small new potatoes
  15ml/1 tbsp chopped fresh rosemary
  15ml/1 tbsp fresh thyme leaves
  1.2 litres/2 pints/5 cups fish stock
  30ml/2 tbsp chopped fresh flat leaf
    parsley leaves
  salt and ground black pepper
  rosemary sprigs, to garnish
  salad leaves and French bread,
    to serve

1 Cut the octopus into large pieces, put in a pan and pour over enough cold water to cover. Season with salt, bring to the boil, then lower the heat and simmer for 30 minutes to tenderize it. Drain and cut into bitesize pieces.

2 Heat the oil in a large shallow pan. Fry the onion until lightly coloured, then add the garlic and fry for 1 minute. Add the octopus and fry for 2–3 minutes, stirring, until coloured.

3 Pour the brandy over the octopus and ignite it. When the flames have died down, add the wine, bring to the boil and bubble gently for about 5 minutes. Stir in the chopped tomatoes, with the chilli and paprika, then add the potatoes, rosemary and thyme. Simmer gently for 5 minutes.

4 Pour in the fish stock and season. Cover and simmer for 20–30 minutes, stirring occasionally, until the octopus and potatoes are tender and the sauce has thickened slightly.

5 To serve, check the seasoning and stir in the parsley. Garnish with rosemary and accompany with salad and bread.

COOK'S TIPS
• Octopus skin can be removed with salted fingers. Large octopus often have scaly rings inside the suckers. Run your fingers down the tentacles to pop out.
• You can make this dish the day before. Simply leave to cool, then chill. To serve, reheat gently, then check the seasoning and stir in the parsley.

MARMITAKO

THIS IS A TRADITIONAL FISHERMAN'S STEW, OFTEN MADE AT SEA, WITH MEATY TUNA STEAKS. THE SUBSTANTIAL FISH IS WONDERFULLY BALANCED BY SWEET PEPPERS AND CIDER, ALL TOPPED BY POTATOES. IT TAKES ITS NAME FROM THE COOKING POT, KNOWN IN FRANCE AS A "MARMITE". TRADITIONALLY A ONE-POT DISH, IT SPEEDS THINGS ALONG TO FRY THE FISH SEPARATELY.

SERVES FOUR

INGREDIENTS
  60ml/4 tbsp olive oil
  1 onion, chopped
  2 garlic cloves, finely chopped
  3 green (bell) peppers, seeded
    and chopped
  ½ dried hot chilli, seeded
    and chopped
  4 light tuna or bonito steaks,
    about 150g/5oz each
  400g/14oz can tomatoes with juice
  10ml/2 tsp paprika
  3 potatoes, diced
  350ml/12fl oz/1½ cups dry
    (hard) cider
  salt and ground black pepper
  30ml/2 tbsp chopped fresh parsley,
    to garnish

1 Heat half the oil in a shallow flameproof casserole big enough to take the fish. Fry the onion gently until softened, then add the garlic. Add the peppers and chilli and stir-fry gently.

2 Season the fish steaks. Heat the remaining oil in a frying pan and fry the fish steaks for 2 minutes on each side over a high heat. Add the tomatoes to the casserole and stir-fry briefly. Add the paprika, then salt and pepper to taste.

VARIATION
Veal steaks or chops can be cooked in the same way. Fry for 5 minutes on each side in step 2, then continue as with fish.

3 Slip the fish steaks into the sauce, moving the peppers into the spaces between them. Cover with the potatoes, pushing them as flat as possible. Add the cider and bring to a simmer. Cover and cook very gently for about 45 minutes, or until the potatoes are done. Check the seasoning, sprinkle with the chopped parsley and serve immediately, straight from the casserole.

ZARZUELA

THE NAME OF THIS DISH TRANSLATES AS "LIGHT MUSICAL COMEDY", REFLECTING THE COLOUR AND VARIETY OF THE STEW, WHICH IS FULL OF ALL SORTS OF FISH AND SHELLFISH. IT IS DISTINGUISHED FROM OTHER FISH STEWS BY CONTAINING TOMATO AS WELL AS SAFFRON. IT'S A SPLENDID FEAST AND NOT DIFFICULT TO MAKE. IF YOUR PAN IS LARGE ENOUGH, INVITE MORE GUESTS AND SIMPLY ADD A LOBSTER, A GOOD PIECE OF HAKE, ANOTHER BASS AND MORE PRAWNS, COCKLES AND OTHER SHELLFISH. TO DRINK, CHOOSE A BOTTLE OF TORRES GRAN VIÑA SOL.

SERVES SIX

INGREDIENTS
  250g/9oz monkfish on the bone
  1 gurnard, snapper or other whole
    white fish, about 350g/12oz
  1 sole, plaice or flounder or
    other whole flat fish, about
    500g/1¼lb, cleaned
  60ml/4 tbsp olive oil
  8 small squid, with tentacles
  plain (all-purpose) flour, for dusting
  30ml/2 tbsp anis spirit, such as
    Ricard or Pernod
  450g/1lb mussels, cleaned
  250ml/8fl oz/1 cup white wine
  4 large scampi (extra large shrimp),
    with heads, uncooked
  12 raw king prawns (jumbo shrimp),
    with heads
  115g/4oz prawns (shrimp)
  salt and ground black pepper
  45ml/3 tbsp chopped fresh parsley,
    to garnish
For the stock
  1 onion, chopped
  1 celery stick, chopped
  1 bay leaf
For the fish broth
  30ml/2 tbsp oil
  1 large onion, finely chopped
  2 garlic cloves, finely chopped
  500g/1¼lb ripe tomatoes, peeled,
    seeded and chopped
  2 bay leaves
  1 dried chilli, seeded
    and chopped
  5ml/1 tsp paprika
  pinch of saffron threads (0.2g)
  salt and ground black pepper

1 Prepare the fish. Remove the flesh from the bones and cut into portions. You should have about 500g/1¼lb white fish, both firm and soft. Salt the fish and reserve on a plate in the refrigerator. (Reserve the bones and heads for making the stock.)

2 Make the stock. Put the onion, celery, bay leaf and the fish bones and heads in a pan, pour in 600ml/1 pint/2½ cups water, and bring to the boil, then simmer for about 30 minutes.

3 Make the broth in a large flameproof casserole. Heat the oil and fry the onion and garlic gently until soft. Add the chopped tomatoes, bay leaves, dried chilli, paprika and crumbled saffron and cook gently to make a sauce.

4 To cook the fish and shellfish, heat the oil in a large frying pan. Put in the squid tentacles, face down, and cook for 45 seconds, to make "flowers". Reserve on a plate.

5 Flour and fry the monkfish and white fish for 3 minutes on each side, then the flat fish for 2 minutes on each side. Cut the squid bodies into rings and fry. Pour the anis spirit into a ladle, flame it and pour over the fish remaining in the pan. Remove the fish and reserve.

6 Strain the fish stock into the casserole and add the wine. Bring to a simmer. Add the mussels in two batches. Cover for a couple of minutes, then remove to a plate, discard any closed mussels, and remove the upper shells.

7 Add the scampi and cook for about 8 minutes, then lift out using a slotted spoon. Cut with scissors along the under side from the head to the tail. Add the raw prawns for 3–4 minutes, then lift out and reserve.

8 About 20 minutes before serving, assemble the casserole. Add the seafood to the hot broth in the following order, bringing the liquid back to simmering each time: firm white fish, soft white fish (with squid rings and pan juices), large shellfish in the shell, cooked shellfish in the shell, then any small shelled prawns. If the liquid level falls below the seafood, make it up with more wine. Check the seasonings.

9 Rearrange the soup with the best-looking shellfish and squid flowers on top. Scatter over the mussels, cover and leave to steam for 2 minutes. Garnish with parsley. Take the casserole to the table with a plate for shells.

COOK'S TIP
Don't leave anything stewing in the broth. Keep the broth warm on a low heat, with the fish at room temperature.

POULTRY AND GAME BIRDS

Chicken was once considered a luxury in Spain and there are many traditional recipes. Try serving chicken with spicy red pepper sauce, with seafood, or with ham and peppers. Other poultry, such as duck, is also on many menus, while game birds are very popular. They may be stuffed with grapes, marinated in wine, cooked with mushrooms or served in delicious sauces.

CHICKEN CHILINDRÓN

This famous chicken dish from Navarre has a spicy red pepper sauce. In the past, the dried choricero pepper – the one that gives chorizos their colour and spice – was used alone, but nowadays the dish is often made with fresh red peppers, spiced with chilli. The name chilindrón *refers to a game of cards. Serve with a* Tempranillo *wine.*

SERVES FOUR

INGREDIENTS
  675g/1½lb red (bell) peppers
  4 free-range chicken portions
  10ml/2 tsp paprika
  30ml/2 tbsp olive oil
  1 large onion, chopped
  2 garlic cloves, finely chopped
  200g/7oz Serrano or other ham, in
    one piece, or a gammon chop
  200g/7oz can chopped tomatoes
  1 dried *guindilla* or other hot
    dried chilli, chopped, or 2.5ml/
    ½ tsp chilli powder, to taste
  salt and ground black pepper
  chopped fresh parsley, to garnish
  small new potatoes, to serve

1 Preheat the grill (broiler) to high. Put the peppers on a baking sheet and grill (broil) for 8–12 minutes, turning occasionally, until the skins have blistered and blackened. Place the blackened peppers in a bowl, cover with clear film (plastic wrap) and leave to cool.

2 Rub salt and paprika into the chicken portions. Heat the oil in a large frying pan and add the chicken portions, skin-side down. Fry over a medium-low heat, turning until golden on all sides.

3 Meanwhile, select a casserole into which the chicken will fit comfortably. Spoon in 45ml/3 tbsp fat from the other pan. Fry the onion and garlic until soft. Dice the ham or gammon and add, stirring occasionally, for a few minutes.

4 Add the chopped tomatoes to the casserole, with the chopped dried chilli or chilli powder. Cook for 4–5 minutes, letting the sauce reduce.

5 Peel the skins off the peppers and discard these and the stalks. Put the peppers into a blender and strain in the juices, discarding the seeds. Process, then add the purée to the casserole and stir in. Heat through.

6 Add the chicken pieces to the casserole, bedding them down in the sauce. Cook, covered, for 15 minutes and check the seasonings, adding more if necessary. Garnish with a little parsley and serve with small new potatoes.

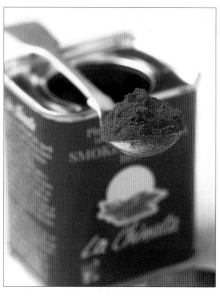

ARROZ CON POLLO

MANY SPANISH FAMILIES EAT RICE ONCE A WEEK, REFERRING TO IT AS ARROZ UNLESS IT IS PAELLA.
RICE WITH CHICKEN IS A CASSEROLE, WITH MORE LIQUID THAN A PAELLA. SEASONAL VEGETABLES
ARE INCLUDED AND EVEN PEAS AND CORN CAN BE USED.

SERVES FOUR

INGREDIENTS

   60ml/4 tbsp olive oil
   6 chicken thighs, free-range if
     possible, halved along the bone
   5ml/1 tsp paprika
   1 large Spanish (Bermuda) onion,
     roughly chopped
   2 garlic cloves, finely chopped
   1 chorizo sausage, sliced
   115g/4oz Serrano or cooked ham
     or gammon, diced
   1 red (bell) pepper, seeded and
     roughly chopped
   1 yellow (bell) pepper, seeded and
     roughly chopped
   225g/8oz/1 generous cup paella rice,
     washed and drained
   2 large tomatoes, chopped or
     200g/7oz can chopped tomatoes
   120ml/4fl oz/½ cup amontillado
     sherry
   750ml/1¼ pints/3 cups
     chicken stock
   5ml/1 tsp dried oregano or thyme
   1 bay leaf
   salt and ground black pepper
   15 green olives and chopped fresh
     flat leaf parsley, to garnish

1 Heat the oil in a wide flameproof casserole. Season the chicken pieces with salt and paprika. Fry until nicely brown all over, then reserve on a plate.

2 Add the onion and garlic to the pan and fry gently until beginning to soften. Add the chorizo and ham or gammon and stir-fry. Add the chopped peppers. Cook until they begin to soften.

3 Sprinkle in the drained rice and cook, stirring, for 1–2 minutes. Add the tomatoes, sherry, chicken stock and dried herbs and season well. Arrange the chicken pieces deep in the mixture, and tuck in the bay leaf.

4 Cover and cook over a very low heat for 30–40 minutes, until the chicken and rice are done. Stir, then garnish and serve.

POLLO CON LANGOSTINOS

CHICKEN WITH PRAWNS IS ANOTHER GORGEOUS CATALAN DISH. THE SAUCE IS THICKENED WITH A PICADA OF GROUND TOASTED ALMONDS, WHICH IS MORE CONVENIENT THAN MAKING A ROUX WITH BUTTER AND FLOUR AT THE LAST MOMENT. THIS SPECIAL PICADA TRADITIONALLY INCLUDES CRUMBLED BUTTER BISCUITS, WHICH WERE CONSIDERED MORE SOPHISTICATED THAN THE BREAD THAT NORMALLY GOES INTO PICADA. THE SAUCE IS FINISHED WITH CREAM AND CAYENNE, AS A MODERN TOUCH — A SPLENDID DINNER-PARTY DISH. SERVE WITH A GLASS OF TORRES GRAN VIÑA SOL.

SERVES FOUR

INGREDIENTS

    1.3kg/3lb free-range chicken
    75–90ml/5–6 tbsp olive oil
    1 large onion, chopped
    2 garlic cloves, finely chopped
    400g/14oz tomatoes, peeled and
      seeded then chopped or 400g/14oz
      can tomatoes, drained
    1 bay leaf
    150ml/¼ pint/⅔ cup dry white wine
    450g/1lb large raw prawns (shrimp),
      or 16 large shelled prawn tails
    15g/½oz/1 tbsp butter
    30ml/2 tbsp anis spirit, such as
      Ricard or Pernod
    75ml/2½fl oz/⅓ cup double
      (heavy) cream
    1.5ml/¼ tsp cayenne pepper
    salt, paprika and ground
      black pepper
    fresh flat leaf parsley, to garnish
    boiled rice or raw spinach salad,
      to serve
For the *picada*
    25g/1oz/¼ cup blanched almonds
    15g/½oz/1 tbsp butter
    1 garlic clove, finely chopped
    3 Marie, Rich Tea or plain all-butter
      biscuits (cookies), broken
    90ml/6 tbsp chopped fresh parsley

1 Cut the chicken into eight serving portions, then separate the small fillet from the back of each breast portion. Rub salt and paprika into the chicken.

2 Heat 30ml/2 tbsp oil in a wide flameproof casserole and fry the onion and garlic until soft. Put in the chicken pieces, skin downwards, and fry over a medium heat, turning until they are golden on all sides.

3 Meanwhile, make the *picada*. Dry-fry the almonds in a small frying pan, shaking it regularly, until they are just coloured. Transfer them to a blender.

4 Add 15g/½oz/1 tbsp butter to the pan and gently fry the garlic, then add it to the blender, with the broken biscuits. Reduce the biscuits to crumbs then add the chopped parsley and blend to a purée, adding a little of the wine intended for the casserole.

5 Add the tomatoes to the casserole, tuck in the bay leaf and cook down to a sauce, stirring occasionally. Pour in the remaining wine, season to taste with salt and ground black pepper, and leave to simmer gently.

6 Check the shelled prawn tails, if using: if they have a black thread along the back, nick it out with a knife. Heat 15ml/1 tbsp oil and the 15g/½oz/1 tbsp butter in the frying pan and add the prawns. Cook over a medium heat for 2 minutes on each side.

7 Pour the anis spirit into a ladle and set light to it. Off the heat pour this over the prawns and let it burn off. Stir in the juices from the casserole, then add the pan contents to the casserole.

8 Remove the bay leaf from the pan and stir in the *picada*, then the cream. Add cayenne to taste and check the seasonings, adding a little more if necessary. Heat through gently and serve garnished with more parsley.

VARIATIONS
The classic version of this dish is beef fillet with lobster. Also try veal with scampi, or partridge with large prawns, for equally delicious results.

BRAISED QUAIL WITH WINTER VEGETABLES

QUAIL ARE BOTH PLENTIFUL AND VERY POPULAR IN SPAIN, ESPECIALLY DURING THE HUNTING SEASON, WHEN EVERY MAN TURNS OUT WITH A GUN, A DOG AND A KNAPSACK. ROASTING AND BRAISING ARE THE TWO CLASSIC TECHNIQUES FOR COOKING QUAIL. HERE, IN CORDONICES ESTOFADAS, THEY ARE COOKED AND SERVED IN A RED WINE SAUCE, THEN ELEGANTLY DISPLAYED ON CRISP CROÛTES.

4 Add more olive oil to the casserole with all the vegetables and shallots. Cook until just colouring. Return the quail to the casserole, breast-sides down, and pour in the red wine. Cover the casserole and transfer to the oven. Cook for about 30 minutes, or until the quail are tender.

5 Meanwhile, make the croûtes. Using a 10cm/4in plain cutter stamp out rounds from the bread. Heat the oil in a frying pan and cook the bread over a high heat until golden on both sides. Drain on kitchen paper and keep warm.

6 Place the croûtes on heated plates and set a quail on top of each one. Arrange the vegetables around the quail, cover and keep hot.

7 Boil the cooking juices hard until reduced to a syrupy consistency. Add the brandy and warm through, then season the sauce with salt and black pepper to taste. Drizzle the sauce over the quail and garnish with parsley, then serve immediately.

SERVES FOUR

INGREDIENTS
  4 quail, cleaned
  175g/6oz small carrots, scrubbed
  175g/6oz baby turnips
  60ml/4 tbsp olive oil
  4 shallots, halved
  450ml/¾ pint/scant 2 cups red wine
  30ml/2 tbsp Spanish brandy
  salt and ground black pepper
  fresh flat leaf parsley, to garnish
For the croûtes
  4 slices stale bread, crusts removed
  60ml/4 tbsp olive oil

1 Preheat the oven to 220°C/425°F/Gas 7. Season the quail with salt and freshly ground black pepper.

2 Using a sharp knife, cut the carrots and baby turnips into chunks. (If the carrots are very small, you can leave them whole if you prefer.)

3 Heat half the olive oil in a flameproof casserole and add the quail. Fry until browned all over, using two wooden spoons or a pair of tongs to turn the birds. Remove from the casserole and set aside.

MARINATED PIGEON IN RED WINE

GREAT CLOUDS OF MIGRATING PIGEONS FLY OVER THE MOUNTAINS OF SPAIN TWICE A YEAR, AND SHOOTING THEM IS A BIG SPORT. HERE THEY ARE MARINATED IN SPICED VINEGAR AND RED WINE, THEN COOKED IN THE MARINADE. REARED SQUAB CAN ALSO BE USED. CABBAGE IS A FAMILIAR PARTNER TO PIGEON, BUT PURÉED CELERIAC ALSO GOES VERY WELL.

SERVES FOUR

INGREDIENTS

    4 pigeons (squabs), each weighing
      about 225g/8oz, cleaned
    30ml/2 tbsp olive oil
    1 onion, roughly chopped
    225g/8oz/3 cups brown cap (cremini)
      mushrooms, sliced
    plain (all-purpose) flour, for dusting
    300ml/½ pint/1¼ cups beef or
      game stock
    30ml/2 tbsp chopped fresh parsley
    salt and ground black pepper
    fresh flat leaf parsley, to garnish
For the marinade
    15ml/1 tbsp olive oil
    1 onion, chopped
    1 carrot, chopped
    1 celery stick, chopped
    3 garlic cloves, sliced
    6 allspice berries, bruised
    2 bay leaves
    8 black peppercorns, bruised
    120ml/4fl oz/½ cup red wine vinegar
    150ml/¼ pint/⅔ cup red wine

1 Starting a day ahead, combine all the ingredients for the marinade in a large dish. Add the pigeons and turn them in the marinade, then cover and chill for 12 hours, turning occasionally.

VARIATION
If you are unable to buy pigeon, this recipe works equally well with rabbit or hare. Buy portions and make deep slashes in the flesh so that the marinade soaks in and flavours right to the centre.

2 Preheat the oven to 150°C/300°F/ Gas 2. Heat the oil in a large, flameproof casserole and cook the onion and mushrooms for about 5 minutes, until the onion has softened.

3 Meanwhile, remove the pigeons to a plate with a slotted spoon and strain the marinade into a bowl, then set both aside separately.

4 Sprinkle the flour on the pigeons and add them to the casserole, breast-sides down. Pour in the marinade and stock, and add the chopped parsley and seasoning. Cover and cook for 1½ hours or until tender.

5 Check the seasoning, then serve the pigeons on warmed plates with the sauce. Garnish with parsley.

PECHUGAS DE PICHONES CON SETAS

PIGEONS ARE CAUGHT IN NETS AS THEY COME SKIMMING THROUGH THE MOUNTAIN PASSES. THE SPORT COMBINES WELL WITH MUSHROOM PICKING – ANOTHER SPANISH DIVERSION. USE THE STRONGEST-FLAVOURED MUSHROOMS YOU CAN FIND. THE PIGEON BREASTS ARE COOKED IN THEIR OWN RICH SAUCE, THEN ELEGANTLY DISPLAYED ON THE SERVING DISH.

SERVES SIX

INGREDIENTS

  6 pigeons (or squabs), cleaned
  90ml/6 tbsp olive oil
  1 large onion, chopped
  2 garlic cloves, finely chopped
  450g/1lb/6 cups brown cap (cremini)
    or small open cap field (portabello)
    mushrooms (use wild mushrooms,
    if possible)
  150g/5oz Serrano or other
    ham, diced
  150ml/¼ pint/⅔ cup red wine
  salt and ground black pepper
  60ml/4 tbsp chopped fresh parsley,
    to garnish
  fried potatoes, to serve
For the stock
  1 large onion, unpeeled,
    roughly chopped
  2 carrots, roughly chopped
  1 celery stick, roughly chopped
  6 tough parsley stalks, snapped
    or bruised
  1 bay leaf
  1 garlic clove, unpeeled but smashed
  4 sprigs of fresh thyme
  12 black peppercorns, crushed

1 First prepare the pigeons. Find the wishbone by pushing your forefinger and thumb in the neck end. It runs up each side; snap it out. Once this is gone, it is easy to take off the breast portions. Cut down on one side of the breastbone with a large knife, then scrape along the rib cage, to get the breast meat off whole. Repeat this, and season the meat.

2 Cut the pigeon carcasses across the ribs and flatten them in a large pan. Add all the stock ingredients and just cover with water. Simmer gently for about 1½ hours to make a rich dark stock. Allow to cool slightly, then strain into a large bowl.

3 Heat 30ml/2 tbsp of the olive oil in a large shallow flameproof casserole and fry the onion and garlic gently for a few minutes, until soft. Meanwhile, pull the mushroom stalks out of the caps, then chop the stalks finely and add to the casserole, with the ham cubes. Fry briefly, stirring. Pour in the wine and 250ml/8fl oz/1 cup of the stock. Simmer gently to reduce a little.

COOK'S TIP
The Spanish definitely prefer wild birds – and they are available in abundance while they are in season. Squabs are the same family as pigeons, but are dovecote birds. They are plumper and slightly blander and benefit from this richly flavoured sauce.

4 Heat 30ml/2 tbsp oil in a large frying pan. Put the pigeon breasts in the pan, skin downward and fry for 2 minutes on each side. Remove to the casserole and simmer for 2–3 minutes.

5 Fry the mushroom caps, in 30ml/ 2 tbsp oil, in the same pan. Arrange the breasts in a ring on an oval platter. Pile the mushrooms in the centre. Spoon the ham and sauce over the pigeon, and sprinkle with parsley.

GUINEA FOWL <u>WITH</u> SAFFRON <u>AND</u> NUT SAUCE

THE ARABS INTRODUCED SAFFRON TO SPAIN AND THIS IS A MOORISH SAUCE, OF SAFFRON, TOASTED ALMONDS GROUND WITH PARSLEY AND SEVERAL SPICES. PEPITA IS THE SPANISH WORD FOR A SEED OR NUT, HENCE THE NAME PINTADA EN PEPITORIA. SERVE WITH A RIOJA RESERVA, TO DRINK.

3 Cut the bird into eight serving pieces, discarding the wing tips, backbone, breastbones and leg tips. This will give you two legs (split them at the joint), two wings with one-third of the breast attached, and two short breast pieces.

4 Heat the olive oil in a wide shallow flameproof casserole and fry the bread slice on both sides. Fry the garlic quickly, then remove both to a blender.

5 Season the poultry well and fry them, turning until golden on all sides. Add the remaining stock and the sherry to the pan, stirring to deglaze the pan. Add the bay leaf and thyme and cover. Cook gently for 10 minutes.

6 Grind together the bread, garlic and almonds. Add the parsley, saffron liquid, nutmeg and cloves, and purée. Stir into the poultry juices, add the lemon juice and paprika, season and serve.

SERVES FOUR

INGREDIENTS
25g/1oz/¼ cup blanched almonds
pinch of saffron threads (0.1g)
120ml/8 tbsp chicken stock
1.2–1.3kg/2½–3lb guinea fowl
60ml/4fl oz/½ cup olive oil
1 thick slice of bread, without crusts
2 garlic cloves, finely chopped
120ml/4fl oz/½ cup fino sherry
1 bay leaf, crumbled
4 thyme sprigs
15ml/1 tbsp finely chopped
  fresh parsley
pinch of freshly grated nutmeg
pinch of ground cloves
juice of ½ lemon
5ml/1 tsp paprika
salt and ground black pepper

1 Preheat the oven to 150°C/300°F/ Gas 2. Spread the almonds on a baking sheet and toast in the oven for about 20 minutes until golden brown.

2 Crumble the saffron with your fingers into a jug (pitcher) or small bowl, pour over 30ml/2 tbsp hot chicken stock and leave to soak.

PERDICES CON UVAS

PARTRIDGES ARE SPAIN'S COMMONEST GAME BIRDS. THEY HAVE A NATURAL AFFINITY WITH GRAPES, AS WILD BIRDS OFTEN ATTACK THE HARVEST. GAME HENS OR ANY PLUMP SMALL BIRD CAN BE USED FOR THIS POT ROAST, WHERE GRAPES ARE USED FOR THE GARNISH AND THE SAUCE.

SERVES FOUR

INGREDIENTS

4 partridges, cleaned
500g/1¼lb red grapes, split and
   seeded, plus extra to garnish
45–60ml/3–4 tbsp olive oil
4 rashers (slices) smoked streaky
   (fatty) bacon, halved across
1 onion, chopped
2 garlic cloves, finely chopped
1 bay leaf
120ml/4fl oz/½ cup dry white wine
250ml/8fl oz/1 cup game or
   chicken stock
freshly grated nutmeg
salt and ground black pepper
30ml/2 tbsp chopped fresh parsley,
   to garnish

2 Fry the bacon until crisp, then reserve on a plate. Put the birds into the casserole breast sides down and fry until coloured. Turn them with two spoons, frying and turning until brown all over. Remove.

3 Fry the onion and garlic, adding a little more oil if needed, until softened.

4 Return the birds to the casserole and arrange two pieces of bacon on top of each. Push 125g/5oz grapes in round them, and add the bay leaf. Pour in the white wine and stock. Add plenty of black pepper. Simmer, covered, for 30 minutes.

5 Remove the birds and bacon to a plate. Spoon the casserole contents into a food processor, discarding the bay leaf, and purée. Add plenty of nutmeg and check the seasoning.

6 Return the birds to the pan, pour the sauce around them, and add 125g/5oz grapes. Heat through. Serve, garnished with extra grapes, crumbled bacon and a little parsley.

1 Season the birds inside and out, then stuff with 250g/9oz grapes. Put 45ml/ 3 tbsp oil in a flameproof casserole into which the birds will fit snugly.

SPICED DUCK WITH PEARS

THIS CATALAN SPECIALITY, KNOWN AS ÀNEC AMB PERES IN THE LOCAL LANGUAGE, IS A FABULOUS COMBINATION OF POULTRY AND FRUIT. DUCKS ARE NOT COMMON IN OTHER REGIONS OF SPAIN. TRY TO BUY A BARBARY DUCK IF YOU CAN. THIS DISH FEATURES THE PICADA, A GREAT CATALAN INVENTION MADE OF POUNDED NUTS, WHICH BOTH FLAVOURS AND THICKENS THE FINAL SAUCE. SERVE WITH A BOTTLE OF GRAN SANGRE DE TORO, WHICH WILL STAND UP WELL TO THIS ROBUSTLY FLAVOURED DISH.

SERVES SIX

INGREDIENTS

   6 duck portions, preferably Barbary,
     either breast or leg pieces
   15ml/1 tbsp olive oil
   1 large onion, thinly sliced
   1 cinnamon stick, halved
   4 thyme sprigs
   475ml/16fl oz/2 cups duck
     or chicken stock
   3 firm, ripe pears
   30ml/2 tbsp olive oil
   25g/1oz/¼ cup raisins
   salt and ground black pepper
   young thyme sprigs or fresh parsley,
     to garnish
   mashed potatoes and green
     vegetables, to serve (optional)
For the *picada*
   30ml/2 tbsp olive oil
   ½ slice stale bread, without crusts
   2 garlic cloves, sliced
   15g/½oz/12 almonds, toasted
   15g/½oz/12 hazelnuts, toasted
   15ml/1 tbsp chopped fresh parsley
   salt and ground black pepper

1 Preheat the oven to 180°C/350°F/ Gas 4. Season the duck portions, pricking the skins with a fork. Fry them, skin side down, for about 5 minutes, until they give off fat. Turn them over and fry on the other side more briefly.

2 Transfer the duck to an ovenproof dish and drain off all but 15ml/1 tbsp of the fat left in the pan.

3 Add the onion to the pan and fry for 5 minutes. Add the cinnamon, thyme and stock and bring to the boil. Pour over the duck, reserving a little of the stock, and bake for 1¼ hours.

4 Make the *picada*. Heat the olive oil in a frying pan and fry the bread over a high heat. Drain on kitchen paper and reserve. Briefly fry the garlic and reserve with the bread.

5 Put all the nuts in a mortar and pound, or reduce to a paste in a food processor or blender. Add the bread, torn into pieces, and the garlic, and reduce to a thick, smooth paste with a little pan stock. Add the parsley and seasoning.

COOK'S TIP
A good stock is essential for this dish. Buy a large duck (plus two extra duck breasts if you want the portions to be generous) and joint it yourself, using the giblets and carcass for stock. Alternatively, buy duck portions and a carton of chicken stock.

6 Peel, core and halve the pears. Fry quickly in the oil in the frying pan until beginning to colour on the cut sides.

7 Add the *picada* to the ovenproof dish with the raisins and pears. Bake for a further 15 minutes until the pears are tender. Season to taste and garnish with thyme or parsley. Serve with mashed potatoes and vegetables, if you wish.

MEAT AND FURRED GAME

There is an impressive variety of meat available in Spain and there are meat and game dishes for every occasion. Try the daily lunch staple, pork empanada, a spring stew of veal with young vegetables, a lamb dish with peppers and Rioja, or classic pulse dishes such as fabada and cocido. Stewed oxtail is a traditional favourite, while rabbit in garlic sauce is a recipe dating back to before Roman times.

FABADA

This bean and sausage hotpot from the wild mountains of Asturias on the northern coast of Spain, has achieved world fame. It used to contain dried broad (fava) beans, which gave it the name, but when these old-fashioned beans were abandoned and modern fabes — white kidney beans — were adopted, it became a truly great dish. Cured sausages, a pork knuckle and belly pork lend the beans an incredible richness, which is enhanced by saffron and paprika. It is a good dish for winter evenings, served with glasses of cider.

SERVES EIGHT

INGREDIENTS
    500–800g/1¼–1¾ lb belly pork,
        in thick slices
    1 smoked gammon (smoked or cured
        ham) knuckle, about 675g/1½ lb,
        skin slashed
    800g/1¾ lb dried cannellini beans,
        soaked overnight (see Cook's Tip)
    5ml/1 tsp black peppercorns, crushed
    15ml/1 tbsp paprika
    pinch of saffron threads (0.2g)
    1 bay leaf
    30ml/2 tbsp oil (optional)
    4 garlic cloves, chopped
    3 red chorizo sausages, thickly sliced
    175g/6oz *morcilla* or black
        pudding (blood sausage),
        thickly sliced
    ground black pepper (optional)

1 Using a very large stockpot (with a capacity of at least 6 litres/10 pints/ 25 cups), put the pork belly and knuckle into the pot with water to cover. Bring to the boil, then drain the meat and return it to the stockpot.

COOK'S TIP
The quality of the bean is a feature of the dish so try to use luxury Spanish beans, now widely exported. *Fabes* are like very large, white cannellini beans. If luxury Spanish beans are unavailable use *lingots* (the French *cassoulet* bean) or large white kidney beans.

2 Add the drained beans to the pot and pour over 2.3 litres/4 pints/10 cups water. Bring to the boil very slowly, then boil for 10 minutes. Reduce the heat and add the peppercorns, paprika, crumbled saffron and the bay leaf.

3 Simmer very gently over a very low heat for 2 hours. (It is best to put the pot over a small burner, turned low.) Check occasionally that the beans are still covered with liquid, but do not stir energetically or the beans will break up.

4 Remove the pork belly and knuckle and set them aside to cool. Strip off the skin and fat, and take 30ml/2 tbsp chopped fat for frying (or use oil). Heat this in a frying pan and cook the garlic lightly, then spoon it into the beans.

VARIATION
Most Spanish bean stews are flavoured with meat from the pig and are then enriched with pork fat. However, in the north, beans are cooked with clams.

5 Fry the chorizo and *morcilla* or black pudding lightly in the same pan. Gently stir into the bean pot.

6 Remove all the meat from the ham bone. Chop it with the pork and return to the stockpot. Simmer for a few minutes. Check the seasonings (there should be enough salt from the meat already) and serve.

PORK EMPANADA

THIS FLAT, TWO-CRUST GALICIAN PIE IS FAMOUS BECAUSE THERE IS NO OCCASION ON WHICH IT IS NOT SERVED. IT IS FESTIVAL FOOD; IT GREETS THE BOATS OF RETURNING FISHERMEN AND IT IS THE MEN'S LUNCHBOX STAPLE. FILLINGS VARY ENORMOUSLY, AND MAY INCLUDE FISH SUCH AS SARDINES, OR SCALLOPS FOR SPECIAL OCCASIONS. THESE PIES ARE GOOD HOT OR COLD.

SERVES EIGHT

INGREDIENTS

- 75ml/5 tbsp olive oil
- 2 onions, chopped
- 4 garlic cloves, finely chopped
- 1kg/2¼lb boned pork loin, diced
- 175g/6oz smoked gammon (smoked or cured ham) or raw ham, diced
- 3 red chorizo or other spicy sausages (about 300g/11oz)
- 3 (bell) peppers (mixed colours), seeded and chopped
- 175ml/6fl oz/¾ cup white wine
- 200g/7oz can tomatoes
- pinch of saffron threads (0.1g)
- 5ml/1 tsp paprika
- 30ml/2 tbsp chopped fresh parsley
- salt and ground black pepper

For the cornmeal dough
- 250g/9oz cornmeal
- 7g/2 tsp easy-blend (rapid-rise) dried yeast
- 5ml/1 tsp caster (superfine) sugar
- 250g/9oz plain (all-purpose) flour, plus extra for dusting
- 5ml/1 tsp salt
- 200ml/7fl oz/scant 1 cup warm water
- 30ml/2 tbsp oil
- 2 eggs, beaten, plus 1 for the glaze

1 Make the filling. Heat 60ml/4 tbsp oil in a frying pan and fry the onions, adding the garlic when the onions begin to colour. Transfer to a flameproof casserole. Add the pork and gammon or ham to the pan, and fry until coloured, stirring. Transfer to the casserole.

2 Add 15ml/1 tbsp oil, the sausage and the peppers to the pan and fry. Transfer to the casserole. Deglaze the pan with the wine, allowing it to bubble and reduce. Pour into the casserole.

3 Add the tomatoes, saffron, paprika and parsley and season. Cook gently for 20–30 minutes. Leave to cool.

4 Meanwhile make the dough. Put the cornmeal into a food processor. Add the dried yeast with the sugar. Gradually add the flour, salt, water, oil and 2 eggs and beat, to make a smooth soft dough.

5 Turn the dough into a clean bowl, cover with a dish towel and leave in a warm place for 40–50 minutes, to rise.

6 Preheat the oven to 200°C/400°F/Gas 6. Grease a shallow roasting pan or dish 30 × 20cm/12 × 8in. Halve the dough. Roll out one half on a floured surface, a little larger than the pan. Lift this in place, leaving the border hanging over the edge.

7 Spoon in the filling. Roll out the lid and lay it in place. Fold the outside edge over the lid (trimming as necessary) and press gently all round with a fork, to seal the pie. Prick the surface and brush with beaten egg.

8 Bake the pie for 30–35 minutes (covering the ends if they brown too much). Cut the pie into squares.

LAMB WITH RED PEPPERS AND RIOJA

WORLD-FAMOUS FOR ITS RED WINE, RIOJA ALSO PRODUCES EXCELLENT RED PEPPERS. IT EVEN HAS A RED PEPPER FAIR, AT LODOSO, EVERY YEAR. TOGETHER THEY GIVE THIS LAMB STEW A LOVELY RICH FLAVOUR. BOILED POTATOES MAKE A VERY GOOD ACCOMPANIMENT.

SERVES FOUR

INGREDIENTS

  15ml/1 tbsp plain (all-purpose) flour
  1kg/2¼lb lean lamb, cubed
  60ml/4 tbsp olive oil
  2 red onions, sliced
  4 garlic cloves, sliced
  10ml/2 tsp paprika
  1.5ml/¼ tsp ground cloves
  400ml/14fl oz/1⅔ cups red Rioja
  150ml/¼ pint/⅔ cup lamb stock
  2 bay leaves
  2 thyme sprigs
  3 red (bell) peppers, halved
   and seeded
  salt and ground black pepper
  bay leaves and thyme sprigs,
   to garnish (optional)

1 Preheat the oven to 160ºC/325ºF/ Gas 3. Season the flour, add the lamb and toss lightly to coat.

2 Heat the oil in a frying pan and fry the lamb until browned. Transfer to an ovenproof dish. Fry the onions and garlic until soft. Add to the meat.

3 Add the paprika, cloves, Rioja, lamb stock, bay leaves and thyme and bring the mixture to a gentle simmer. Add the halved red peppers. Cover the dish with a lid or foil and cook for about 30 minutes, or until the meat is tender. Garnish with more bay leaves and thyme sprigs, if you like.

VEAL CASSEROLE <u>WITH</u> BROAD BEANS

THIS DELICATE STEW, FLAVOURED WITH SHERRY AND PLENTY OF GARLIC, IS A SPRING DISH MADE WITH NEW VEGETABLES — MENESTRA DE TERNERA. FOR A DELICIOUS FLAVOUR BE SURE TO ADD PLENTY OF PARSLEY JUST BEFORE SERVING. LAMB IS EQUALLY GOOD COOKED IN THIS WAY.

SERVES SIX

INGREDIENTS
  45ml/3 tbsp olive oil
  1.3–1.6kg/3–3½lb veal, cut into
    5cm/2in cubes
  1 large onion, chopped
  6 large garlic cloves, unpeeled
  1 bay leaf
  5ml/1 tsp paprika
  240ml/8fl oz/1 cup fino sherry
  100g/4oz/scant 1 cup shelled,
    skinned broad (fava) beans
  60ml/4 tbsp chopped fresh flat
    leaf parsley
salt and ground black pepper

1 Heat 30ml/2 tbsp oil in a large flameproof casserole. Add half the meat and brown well on all sides. Transfer to a plate. Brown the rest of the meat and remove from the pan.

2 Add the remaining oil to the pan and cook the onion until soft. Return the meat to the casserole and stir well to mix with the onion.

3 Add the garlic cloves, bay leaf, paprika and sherry. Season with salt and black pepper. Bring to simmering point, then cover and cook very gently for 30–40 minutes.

4 Add the broad beans to the casserole about 10 minutes before the end of the cooking time. Check the seasoning and stir in the chopped parsley just before serving.

COCIDO

The Spanish national dish, cocido is also Madrid's most famous stew. The name simply means "boiled dinner" and it used to be made more than once a week. A pot of fresh and salt meat with chicken and sausages is simmered with chickpeas and some fresh vegetables. The broth makes a soup course and then the rest is displayed on two splendid platters. Serve with a bottle of Viña Arana from La Rioja Alta or Bodegas Bilbainas Viña Pomal.

SERVES EIGHT

INGREDIENTS
    500–800g/1¼–1¾ lb cured brisket
      or silverside (pot roast)
    250g/9oz smoked streaky (fatty)
      bacon, in one piece, or 250g/9oz
      belly pork
    1 knuckle gammon (smoked or cured
      ham) bone, with some meat
      still attached
    500–750g/1¼–1¾ lb beef marrow
      bone, sawn through
    1 pig's trotter (foot), sawn through
    1 whole garlic bulb
    2 bay leaves
    5ml/1 tsp black peppercorns,
      lightly crushed
    250g/9oz/1¼ cups dried chickpeas,
      soaked overnight and drained
    2 quarters corn-fed chicken
    1 small onion, studded with
      2 or 3 cloves
    2 large carrots, cut into big pieces
    2 leeks, cut into chunks
    500g/1¼ lb small new potatoes,
      scrubbed
    2 red chorizo sausages
    1 *morcilla* or 250g/9oz black pudding
      (blood sausage)
    30ml/2 tbsp long grain rice
    1 small (bell) pepper, finely diced
    salt

1 Put the salt meat – brisket or silverside, bacon or pork and knuckle – into a large pan and cover with water. Bring slowly to the boil, simmer for 5 minutes to remove excess salt, and drain.

VARIATIONS
The types of meat used in this hearty stew can be varied. Just make sure that you include a salty meat, a meat on the bone, a smoked meat, a piece of pork, a piece of beef and a piece of chicken – plus a paprika sausage.

2 Using a very large stockpot (with a capacity of at least 6 litres/10 pints/ 5 quarts), pack in all the meat, skin side down, with the marrowbone and trotter. Add the garlic bulb, bay leaves and peppercorns, with water to cover. Bring to simmering point, skimming off any scum, with a slotted spoon.

3 Add the drained chickpeas, cover and simmer on the lowest possible heat for 1½ hours, checking occasionally that there is enough liquid.

4 Add the chicken and onion to the pot. Cook until the chickpeas are done.

5 Start the vegetables. Put the carrots, leeks and potatoes into a large pan with the chorizo (but not the *morcilla* or black pudding). Cover with water and bring to the boil. Simmer for 25 minutes, until the potatoes are cooked. About 5 minutes before the end, add the *morcilla* or black pudding.

6 Strain off enough broth from the meat pot (about 1.2 litres/2 pints/5 cups) into a pan, for soup. Bring back to the boil, sprinkle in the rice and cook for 15 minutes. Add the diced pepper and cook for 2–3 minutes more. Serve the soup as the first course.

7 Drain the vegetables and sausages and arrange on a platter. Serve as a separate second course or as an accompaniment with the meat.

8 Slice the meats, removing the marrow from the bone and adding it to the chickpeas. Arrange with all the meats on a heated serving platter, moistening with a little broth.

RABO DE TORO

In the Spanish kitchen, the most famous part of the bull is his tail — although most people are more likely to cook with oxtail. Either makes a rich, succulent meat stew, which can be prepared several days ahead, and tastes even better reheated.

SERVES SIX

INGREDIENTS

60ml/4 tbsp olive oil
2 onions, chopped
30ml/2 tbsp plain (all-purpose) flour
1.6kg/3½lb oxtail, chopped across
6 carrots
2 large garlic cloves, smashed
1 bay leaf
2 thyme sprigs
2 leeks, sliced thinly
1 clove
pinch of freshly grated nutmeg
350ml/12fl oz/1½ cups red wine
30ml/2 tbsp vinegar
350ml/12fl oz/1½ cups stock
30ml/2 tbsp fino sherry
60ml/4 tbsp chopped fresh parsley
salt, paprika and black pepper
boiled potatoes, to serve

1 Starting a day ahead, preheat the oven to 150°C/300°F/Gas 2. Heat 30ml/ 2 tbsp oil in a large frying pan, add the onions and fry until softened. Remove to a casserole (in which the oxtail will fit in a single layer).

2 Season the flour with salt, paprika and pepper and dust the oxtail pieces all over. Add the remaining oil to the pan and put in the oxtail pieces, on their sides at first. Fry, turning them to brown all over, then fit them into the casserole, standing upright.

3 Cut the carrots into short lengths and push into the spaces between the pieces of oxtail in the casserole. Tuck in the garlic cloves, bay leaf and thyme sprigs and add the sliced leeks.

4 Add the clove, grated nutmeg and more black pepper. Pour in the wine, vinegar and just enough stock to cover. Bring to simmering point, then cover the casserole with a lid and put in the oven. Cook for about 3 hours, or until the meat is falling off the bones.

5 Skim the fat off the top of the stew. Spoon the larger meat pieces on to a plate and remove the bones and fat.

6 Push all the remaining oxtail and the carrots to one end of the pan and discard the bay leaf and thyme. Spoon the garlic and some of the soft vegetables into a food processor and purée with the sherry. Return the meat and purée to the casserole and heat through. Stir in the parsley, check the seasonings and serve with boiled potatoes.

RABBIT SALMOREJO

THE CARTHAGINIANS NAMED SPAIN "RABBIT LAND" (AFTER SPHAN, RABBIT) AND THE ROMANS KEPT THE NAME, REFERRING TO THE COUNTRY AS HISPANIA. THE MODERN NAME, ESPAÑA, IS CLEARLY DERIVED FROM THIS OLD NAME AND SERVES TO REMIND US HOW COMMON RABBITS ARE THROUGHOUT SPAIN. THIS IS AN UPDATED VERSION OF ONE OF THE CLASSIC MEDITERRANEAN RABBIT STEWS. SALMOREJO INDICATES POUNDED GARLIC, BREAD AND VINEGAR, WHILE WINE IS A MODERN TOUCH.

SERVES FOUR

INGREDIENTS
675g/1½lb rabbit, jointed
300ml/½ pint/1¼ cups dry
    white wine
15ml/1 tbsp sherry vinegar
several oregano sprigs
2 bay leaves
30ml/2 tbsp plain (all-purpose) flour
90ml/6 tbsp olive oil
175g/6oz baby (pearl) onions,
    peeled and left whole
4 garlic cloves, sliced
150ml/¼ pint/⅔ cup chicken stock
1 dried chilli, seeded and
    finely chopped
10ml/2 tsp paprika
salt and ground black pepper
fresh flat leaf parsley sprigs,
    to garnish (optional)

1 Put the rabbit in a bowl. Add the wine, vinegar, oregano and bay leaves and toss together. Marinate for several hours or overnight in the refrigerator.

2 Drain the rabbit, reserving the marinade, and pat it dry with kitchen paper. Season the flour and use to dust the marinated rabbit.

3 Heat the oil in a large, wide flameproof casserole or frying pan. Fry the rabbit pieces until golden on all sides, then remove them and set aside. Fry the onions until they are beginning to colour, then reserve on a separate plate.

4 Add the garlic to the pan and fry, then add the strained marinade, with the chicken stock, chilli and paprika.

5 Return the rabbit and the reserved onions to the pan. Bring to a simmer, then cover and simmer gently for about 45 minutes until the rabbit is tender. Check the seasoning, adding more vinegar and paprika if necessary. Serve the dish garnished with a few sprigs of flat leaf parsley, if you like.

COOK'S TIP
If you wish, rather than cooking on the stove, transfer the stew to an ovenproof dish and bake in the oven at 180°C/350°F/Gas 4 for about 50 minutes.

DESSERTS AND BAKING

Iced desserts were introduced to Spain by the Moors, who also created luxurious dishes of fruit in syrups. Caramel is a much-loved flavour and is used in a drunken cake soaked in brandy. Custards are also popular and come with a crisp caramel topping or baked with a caramel syrup. As well as tempting desserts there are delicious, light breakfast rolls and traditional sweet loaves baked for special occasions.

BITTER CHOCOLATE MOUSSES

THE SPANISH INTRODUCED CHOCOLATE TO EUROPE, AND CHOCOLATE MOUSSE REMAINS A FAVOURITE DESSERT IN A COUNTRY THAT USUALLY FAVOURS CUSTARDS AND FRESH FRUIT. THESE DELICIOUS CREMAS DE CHOCOLATE ARE RICH WITH CHOCOLATE, WITH A HINT OF ORANGE LENT BY THE LIQUEUR.

2 Whip the cream until soft peaks form, then stir a spoonful into the chocolate mixture to lighten it. Gently fold in the remaining whipped cream.

3 In a clean, grease-free bowl, use an electric mixer to slowly whisk the egg whites until frothy. Increase the speed and continue until the egg whites form soft peaks. Gradually sprinkle the sugar over the egg whites and continue beating until the whites are stiff and glossy. (Be careful not to over-whisk the eggs.)

4 Using a rubber spatula or large metal spoon, stir a quarter of the egg whites into the chocolate mixture to lighten it, then gently fold in the remaining whites, cutting down to the bottom of the bowl, along the sides and up to the top in a semicircular motion until they are just combined. Don't worry about a few white streaks.

SERVES EIGHT

INGREDIENTS
  225g/8oz dark (bittersweet)
    chocolate, chopped
  30ml/2 tbsp orange liqueur or a good
    Spanish brandy such as Torres
  50g/2oz/¼ cup unsalted (sweet)
    butter, cut into small pieces
  4 large (US extra large)
    eggs, separated
  90ml/6 tbsp whipping cream
  45ml/3 tbsp caster (superfine) sugar

COOK'S TIP
The addition of 1.5ml/¼ tsp cream of tartar to the egg whites helps them to stabilize and hold the volume.

1 Place the chocolate and 60ml/4 tbsp water in a heavy pan. Melt over a low heat, stirring. Off the heat whisk in the orange liqueur or brandy and butter. Beat the egg yolks until thick and creamy, then slowly beat into the melted chocolate until well blended.

5 Gently spoon the mixture into eight individual dishes or a 2 litre/3½ pint/ 8 cup bowl. Chill for at least 2 hours until set before serving.

FLAN

THESE LITTLE BAKED CARAMEL CUSTARDS, MADE IN BUCKET-SHAPED MOULDS, ARE THE BEST-KNOWN AND MOST POPULAR OF ALL SPANISH DESSERTS. IF YOU DON'T OWN SMALL MOULDS, YOU CAN MAKE ONE LARGE FLAN INSTEAD BUT IT WILL NEED TO BE COOKED FOR A LITTLE LONGER.

SERVES EIGHT

INGREDIENTS
250g/9oz/1¼ cups granulated sugar
1 vanilla pod (bean) or 10ml/2 tsp
  vanilla extract
400ml/14fl oz/1⅔ cups milk
250ml/8fl oz/1 cup whipping cream
5 large (US extra large) eggs
2 egg yolks

1 Select your moulds – eight metal dariole moulds, about 120ml/4fl oz/ ½ cup each, or a soufflé dish 1 litre/ 1¾ pints/4 cups in capacity. Arrange in a roasting pan.

2 Put 175g/6oz/⅞ cup of the sugar in a small heavy pan with 60ml/4 tbsp water. Bring to the boil over a high heat, swirling the pan to dissolve the sugar. Boil, without stirring, for about 5 minutes until the syrup turns a dark caramel colour.

3 If using individual moulds, pour a little caramel into each one. If using a single mould, lift it with oven gloves and quickly swirl the dish to coat the base with the caramel. (The caramel will harden quickly as it cools.)

4 Preheat the oven to 160°C/325°F/ Gas 3. If using, split the vanilla pod lengthways and scrape out the seeds. Pour the milk and cream into a pan, add the vanilla seeds or extract and bring the mixture close to the boil, stirring. Remove from the heat and allow to stand for 15–20 minutes.

5 In a bowl, whisk the eggs and extra yolks with the remaining sugar for 2–3 minutes until creamy. Whisk in the warm milk and cream mixture, and then strain it into the caramel-lined mould(s). Cover with foil.

6 Pour boiling water into the pan, to come halfway up the sides of the mould(s). Bake until the custard is just set (20–25 minutes for small moulds; about 40 minutes for a large one. A knife inserted to test should come out clean.) Remove from the water, leave to cool, then chill overnight.

7 To turn out, run a palette knife around the custard(s). Cover a large mould with a serving dish and, holding tightly, invert the dish and plate together. Lift one edge of the mould, waiting for the caramel to run down, then remove the mould. Cover the small moulds with saucers and invert them to serve.

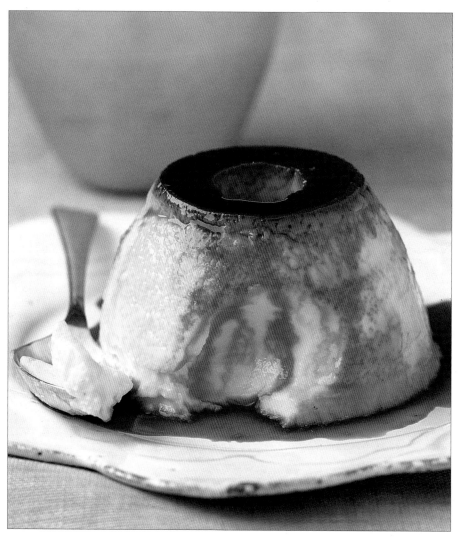

CREMA CATALANA

THIS FABULOUS SPANISH DESSERT OF CREAMY CUSTARD TOPPED WITH A NET OF BRITTLE SUGAR, MAY WELL BE THE ORIGINAL OF ALL CRÈME BRÛLÉES. CREMAT IS THE CATALAN WORD FOR "BURNT", AND THIS WAS PROBABLY PART OF ITS ORIGINAL NAME.

SERVES FOUR

INGREDIENTS
475ml/16fl oz/2 cups milk
pared rind of ½ lemon
1 cinnamon stick
4 large egg yolks
105ml/7 tbsp caster
  (superfine) sugar
25ml/1½ tbsp cornflour (cornstarch)
ground nutmeg, for sprinkling

COOK'S TIP
A special tool known as a *quemadora* is sold to caramelize the top of this dessert. A metal disc on a wooden handle is heated like a hot poker, then held over the sugar crust.

1 Put the milk in a pan with the lemon rind and cinnamon stick. Bring to the boil, then simmer for 10 minutes. Remove the lemon rind and cinnamon. Put the egg yolks and 45ml/3 tbsp sugar in a bowl, and whisk until pale yellow. Add the cornflour and mix well.

2 Stir a few tablespoons of the hot milk into the egg yolk mixture, then tip back into the remaining milk. Return to the heat and cook gently, stirring, for about 5 minutes, until thickened and smooth. Do not boil.

3 Pour the custard into four shallow ovenproof dishes, about 13cm/5in in diameter. Leave to cool, then chill for a few hours, or overnight, until firm.

4 No more than 30 minutes before serving, sprinkle each dessert with 15ml/1 tbsp of the sugar and a little nutmeg. Preheat the grill (broiler) to high. Place the dishes under the grill, on the highest shelf, and cook until the sugar caramelizes. This will only take a few seconds and it will caramelize unevenly. Leave the custards to cool for a few minutes before serving.

ARROPE

THIS IS AN OLD ARAB RECIPE WHOSE NAME MEANS "SYRUP"; THIS VERSION COMES FROM THE PYRENEES REGION. IN SOUTHERN SPAIN, GRAPES, QUINCE AND MELON MIGHT BE USED. ARROPE STARTS AS A LOVELY FRUIT COMPOTE AND ENDS UP AS A SYRUPY JAM, TO BE SCOOPED UP WITH BREAD.

SERVES TEN

INGREDIENTS
  3 firm peaches, unpeeled
  1kg/2¼lb/5 cups granulated sugar
  3 large eating apples
  finely grated rind of 1 lemon
  3 firm pears
  finely grated rind of 1 orange
  1 small sweet potato, 150g/5oz
    prepared weight
  200g/7oz butternut squash, peeled
    and prepared weight
  250ml/8fl oz/1 cup dark rum
  30ml/2 tbsp clear honey

1 Cut the peaches into eighths, without peeling them, and place in the bottom of a large flameproof casserole. Sprinkle with 15ml/1 tbsp of the sugar.

2 Peel and core the apples and cut them into 16 segments, then arrange on top of the peaches. Sprinkle the lemon rind over the top, along with 15ml/1 tbsp of the sugar. Prepare the pears in the same way as the apples, place in the casserole, then sprinkle over the orange rind, followed by 15ml/1 tbsp of the sugar.

3 Slice the sweet potato into pieces half the size of the pears and spread them over the top. Prepare the squash in the same way, layering it on top. Sprinkle about 15ml/1 tbsp of the sugar. Cover with a plate that fits inside the rim, and weigh down with a couple of cans. Stand for a minimum of 2 hours (maximum 12) for juice to form.

4 Remove the cans and plate, put the casserole over a fairly low heat and bring to a simmer. Cook and soften the fruit for 20 minutes, stirring once or twice to prevent sticking.

5 Add the remaining sugar, in three or four batches, stirring to dissolve each batch before adding the next. Bring the mixture up to a rolling boil, over a medium high heat, and boil very steadily for 45 minutes. Stir and lift off any scum.

6 The syrup should be considerably reduced. Test by pouring a spoonful on a plate. It should wrinkle when a spoon is pulled across (like jam in the early stages, before a full set is achieved).

7 Off the heat, add the rum and honey and stir well to combine. Return the casserole to a moderate heat and cook for a further 10 minutes, stirring frequently to prevent the fruit sticking to the base of the pan. The colour will deepen to russet brown. Remove the pan from the heat and set aside to cool.

8 If the resulting compote is a little too stiff, then stir in some more rum before serving.

COOK'S TIP
Arrope is immensely rich, so portions should be small. By the time you reach the bottom of the pot it becomes very thick and sticky, and is best scooped up on bits of bread.

LECHE FRITA WITH BLACK FRUIT SAUCE

THE NAME OF THIS DESSERT MEANS "FRIED MILK", BUT IT IS REALLY CUSTARD SQUARES. IT IS VERY POPULAR IN THE BASQUE COUNTRY, AND HAS A MELTING, CREAMY CENTRE AND CRUNCHY, GOLDEN COATING. HERE, IT IS SERVED HOT WITH A DARK FRUIT SAUCE, BUT IT IS ALSO GOOD COLD.

SERVES SIX TO EIGHT

INGREDIENTS
  550ml/18fl oz/2½ cups full-fat
    (whole) milk
  3 finely pared strips of lemon rind
  ½ cinnamon stick
  90g/3½oz/½ cup caster (superfine)
    sugar, plus extra for sprinkling
  60ml/4 tbsp cornflour (cornstarch)
  30ml/2 tbsp plain (all-purpose) flour
  3 large (US extra large) egg yolks
  2 large (US extra large) eggs
  90–120ml/6–8 tbsp stale
    breadcrumbs or dried crumbs
  sunflower oil, for frying
  ground cinnamon, for dusting
For the sauce
  450g/1lb blackcurrants
    or blackberries
  90g/3½oz/½ cup granulated sugar,
    plus extra for dusting

1 Put the milk, lemon rind, cinnamon stick and sugar in a pan and bring to the boil, stirring gently. Cover and leave to infuse for 20 minutes.

2 Put the cornflour and flour in a bowl and beat in the egg yolks with a wooden spoon. Add a little of the milk and beat to make a smooth batter.

3 Strain the remaining hot milk into the batter, then pour back into the pan. Cook over a low heat, stirring constantly. (The mixture won't curdle, but it will thicken unevenly if you let it.) Cook for a couple of minutes, until it thickens and separates from the side of the pan.

4 Beat the mixture hard with the spoon to ensure a really smooth consistency. Pour into an 18–20cm/7–8in, 1cm/½in-deep rectangular dish, and smooth the top. Cool, then chill until firm.

5 Make the fruit sauce. Cook the blackcurrants or blackberries with the sugar and a little water for about 10 minutes until soft.

6 Reserve 30–45ml/2–3 tbsp whole currants or berries, then put the rest in a food processor and blend to make a smooth purée. Return the purée and berries to the pan.

7 Cut the chilled custard into eight or twelve squares. Beat the eggs in a shallow dish and spread out the breadcrumbs on a plate. Lift half of the squares with a metal spatula into the egg. Coat on both sides, then lift into the crumbs and cover all over. Repeat with the second batch of squares.

8 Pour about 1cm/½in oil into a deep frying pan and heat until very hot.

9 Lift two or three coated squares with a palette knife (metal spatula) into the oil and fry for a couple of minutes, shaking or spooning the oil over the top, until golden. Reserve on kitchen paper, while frying the other batches.

10 To serve, arrange the custard squares on plates and sprinkle with sugar and cinnamon. Pour a circle of warm sauce round the squares, distributing the whole berries evenly.

COOK'S TIP
In Spain, milk is usually drunk at breakfast or used for cheese. In northern Spain, the milk has a wonderful quality and has been given special status as a dessert ingredient. Most popular of all the milk desserts are *leche frita*, *flan* and *filloas* (thin pancakes).

HONEY-BAKED FIGS WITH HAZELNUT ICE CREAM

TWO WILD INGREDIENTS – FIGS AND HAZELNUTS – ARE USED TO MAKE THIS DELECTABLE DESSERT,
HIGOS CON HELADO DE AVELLANA. FRESH FIGS ARE BAKED IN A LIGHTLY SPICED LEMON AND
HONEY SYRUP AND ARE SERVED WITH HOME-MADE ROASTED HAZELNUT ICE CREAM.

SERVES FOUR

INGREDIENTS

   finely pared rind of 1 lemon
   1 cinnamon stick, roughly broken
   60ml/4 tbsp clear honey
   8 large figs
For the hazelnut ice cream
   450ml/¾ pint/scant 2 cups double
     (heavy) cream
   50g/2oz/¼ cup caster
     (superfine) sugar
   3 large (US extra large) egg yolks
   1.5ml/¼ tsp vanilla extract
   75g/3oz/¾ cup hazelnuts

1 Make the ice cream. Gently heat the cream in a pan until almost boiling. Meanwhile, beat the sugar and egg yolks in a bowl until creamy.

2 Pour a little hot cream into the egg yolk mixture and stir with a wooden spoon. Pour back into the pan and mix well. Cook over a low heat, stirring constantly, until the mixture thickens slightly and lightly coats the back of the spoon – do not allow it to boil.

3 Pour the custard into a bowl, stir in the vanilla extract and leave to cool.

4 Preheat the oven to 180°C/350°F/ Gas 4. Place the hazelnuts on a baking sheet and roast for 10–12 minutes, or until golden. Leave the nuts to cool, then grind them in a food processor.

5 If you have an ice cream machine, pour in the cold custard and churn until half set. Add the ground hazelnuts and continue to churn until the ice cream is thick. Freeze until firm.

6 Working by hand, pour the custard into a freezerproof container and freeze for 2 hours, or until the custard feels firm around the edges. Turn into a bowl and beat with an electric whisk or turn into a food processor and beat until smooth. Stir in the hazelnuts and freeze until half set. Beat once more, then freeze until firm.

7 Preheat the oven to 200°C/400°F/ Gas 6. Remove the ice cream from the freezer and allow to soften slightly.

8 To make the syrup, put the lemon rind, cinnamon stick, honey and 200ml/ 7fl oz/scant 1 cup water in a small pan and heat slowly until boiling. Simmer the mixture for 5 minutes, then leave to stand for 15 minutes.

9 Using a sharp knife, cut the figs almost into quarters but leaving the figs still attached at the base. Pack them into a casserole, in a single layer, and pour the honey syrup round and over them. Cover the dish tightly with foil and bake for 10 minutes.

10 Arrange the figs on small serving plates, with the cooking syrup poured round them. Serve accompanied by a scoop or two of the ice cream.

COOK'S TIPS
• When toasting the hazelnuts, keep a close eye on them because they can scorch very quickly, spoiling the flavour of the ice cream.
• In southern Spain, red-fleshed figs with a wonderfully sweet flavour grow wild in the scrub.

BASQUE APPLE TART

TARTA DE MANZANA OR PASTEL VASCO, AS IT IS ALSO KNOWN, IS MADE WITH A HEAVY SWEET PASTRY, WHICH HAS THE TEXTURE AND TASTE OF CAKE. IT OFTEN HAS A CUSTARD CENTRE. THIS ONE HAS AN APPLE FILLING, BUT OTHER FRESH FRUIT, SUCH AS APRICOTS OR PLUMS, WORK JUST AS WELL.

4 Place the larger piece of dough on a lightly floured piece of clear film (plastic wrap) and cover with another piece of film. Roll out to a 25cm/10in round. Remove the top layer of film and lift up the dough on the second film. Place the dough face down in the tin and peel off the film. Press into the tin so that it stands just clear of the top.

5 Pack the tin with the apples and sprinkle with cinnamon. Roll out the second piece of dough in the same way, to exactly the same size as the tin. Lay the dough on top of the apples and fold the overlapping edges of the bottom piece of dough inward. Gently press the edges together with a fork, to seal.

SERVES SIX

INGREDIENTS

215g/7½oz/scant 2 cups plain (all-purpose) flour, plus extra for rolling
5ml/1 tsp baking powder
pinch of salt
115g/4oz/½ cup cold unsalted (sweet) butter, cubed
finely grated rind of ½ lemon
75g/3oz/scant ½ cup caster (superfine) sugar, plus extra for sprinkling
2 small (US medium) eggs
3 eating apples, peeled, cored and cubed
ground cinnamon, for sprinkling
whipped cream, to serve

1 Sift the flour, baking powder and salt into a food processor. Add the butter and grated lemon rind and process briefly to combine, then add the sugar, 1 whole egg and the yolk of the second egg to the flour mixture and process to make a soft dough.

2 Divide the dough into two pieces, one portion nearly double the size of the other. Pat the dough into two flat cakes. Wrap tightly in clear film (plastic wrap) and chill for at least 2 hours until firm.

3 Preheat the oven to 180°C/350°F/ Gas 4. Place a baking sheet in the oven and grease a 20cm/8in loose-based flan tin (tart pan).

6 Prick the dough a few times, brush with egg white and sprinkle with sugar. Place on the hot baking sheet and bake for 20 minutes, then reduce the temperature to 160°C/325°F/Gas 3 for a further 25–30 minutes until golden.

7 Leave the tart to cool in the tin for 30 minutes, then unmould and cool on a wire rack. Serve with whipped cream.

BISCOCHO BORRACHO

THE NAME OF THIS MOIST, NUTTY DESSERT TRANSLATES AS "DRUNKEN CAKE", INDICATING THAT IT IS SOAKED IN BRANDY-FLAVOURED SYRUP. THE CAKE CAN BE LAYERED WITH CREAM, BUT THIS VERSION IS MADE IN A MOULD, THEN TURNED OUT. PIPE WITH WHIPPED CREAM IF YOU LIKE.

SERVES SIX TO EIGHT

INGREDIENTS
    butter, for greasing
    90g/3½oz/¾ cup plain
        (all-purpose) flour
    6 large (US extra large) eggs
    90g/3½oz/½ cup caster
        (superfine) sugar
    finely grated rind of 1 lemon
    90ml/6 tbsp toasted flaked
        almonds
    250ml/8fl oz/1 cup whipping
        cream, to serve
For the syrup
    115g/4oz/generous ½ cup caster
        (superfine) sugar
    120ml/4fl oz/½ cup boiling water
    105ml/7 tbsp Spanish brandy

1 Starting 1–2 days ahead, preheat the oven to 200°C/400°F/Gas 6. Butter a shallow tin (pan), about 28 × 18cm/ 11 × 7in. Line the tin with baking parchment and butter well.

2 Sift the flour a couple of times into a bowl. Separate the eggs, putting the whites into a large bowl. Put the yolks in a food processor with the sugar and lemon rind and beat until light. Whisk the whites to soft peaks, then work a little white into the yolk mixture.

3 Dribble two spoonfuls of the yolk mixture across the whites, sift some flour over the top and cut in gently with a large spoon. Continue folding together in this way until all the egg yolk mixture and flour have been incorporated.

4 Turn the mixture into the prepared tin and smooth over. Bake for 12 minutes. Leave the cake to set for 5 minutes, then turn out on to a wire rack. Peel off the paper and leave to cool completely.

5 Make the syrup. Place 50g/2oz/¼ cup sugar into a small pan and add 15ml/ 1 tbsp water. Heat until it caramelizes, shaking the pan a little if one side starts to brown too fast. As soon as it colours, dip the base of the pan into a bowl of cold water. Add the remaining sugar and pour in the boiling water. Bring back to a simmer, stirring until the sugar has dissolved. Pour into a jug (pitcher) and add the brandy.

6 Put the cake back into the tin and drizzle half the syrup over it. Choose a 700ml/1½ pint/3 cup capacity mould or tin; cut the cake into scallops with a spoon and layer half into the bottom of it. Scatter 30ml/2 tbsp almonds over the top, and push them down the cracks. Top with the remaining cake and nuts.

7 Pour the remaining syrup over the cake, cover with foil and weight down the top. Chill until ready to serve.

8 To serve, whip the cream. Run a knife round the mould and turn the cake out on to a long dish. Scatter with almonds and serve with the cream.

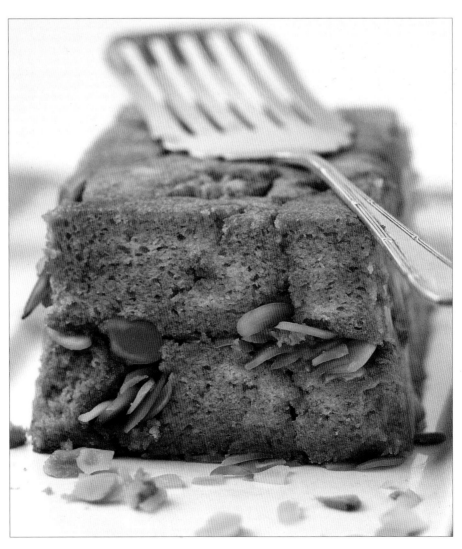

BREAKFAST ENSAIMADAS

ORIGINALLY FROM MALLORCA, THESE SNAIL-SHAPED BUNS, MADE OF THE LIGHTEST POSSIBLE DOUGH, ARE A DELICIOUS TRADITIONAL TREAT. THEY ARE NOW EATEN IN MADRID AND THROUGHOUT SOUTHERN AND EASTERN SPAIN FOR BREAKFAST. TRADITIONALLY LARD OR SAIM, AS IT IS KNOWN IN SPAIN, BRUSHED OVER THE TOPS, BUT NOWADAYS BUTTER IS USED AND ADDS A DELICIOUS RICHNESS.

MAKES SIXTEEN ROLLS

INGREDIENTS
225g/8oz/2 cups unbleached strong
   white bread flour
2.5ml/½ tsp salt
50g/2oz/¼ cup caster
   (superfine) sugar
15g/½oz fresh yeast
75ml/5 tbsp lukewarm milk
1 egg
30ml/2 tbsp sunflower oil
50g/2oz/¼ cup butter, melted
icing (confectioners') sugar,
   for dusting

COOK'S TIP
Coating the dough with butter helps
to separate the coils as they expand.

1 Lightly grease two baking sheets. Sift the flour and salt together in a large mixing bowl and add the sugar.

2 In a small bowl, cream the yeast and lukewarm milk together. Pour the mixture into the centre of the flour, then sprinkle a little of the flour evenly over the top of the liquid. Leave in a warm place for about 15 minutes until frothy.

3 Turn the mixture into a food processor and process briefly to combine. In a small bowl, beat together the egg and sunflower oil, then pour the mixture into the food processor and work to a smooth dough. Process the dough for several minutes, until it becomes smooth and elastic.

4 Put the dough in a lightly oiled bowl, cover with clear film (plastic wrap) and leave to rise, in a warm place, for 1 hour, or until doubled in size.

5 Put the dough in the food processor and use the pulse button to work until smooth. Turn out on to a lightly floured surface and divide into 16 equal pieces.

6 Shape each piece of dough into a thin rope about 38cm/15in long. Pour the melted butter on to a plate and dip each piece of dough into it to coat.

7 On the baking sheets, curl each rope into a loose spiral, spacing them well apart. Tuck the ends under to seal. Cover with clear film and leave to rise, in a warm place, for about 45 minutes, or until doubled in size.

8 Preheat the oven to 190°C/375°F/ Gas 5. Brush the rolls with water and dust with icing sugar. Bake for about 10 minutes, or until light golden brown. Cool on a wire rack. Dust again with icing sugar and serve warm.

TWELFTH NIGHT BREAD

JANUARY 6TH, EPIPHANY, CELEBRATES THE ARRIVAL OF THE THREE KINGS AT CHRIST'S MANGER AND IN SPAIN, IT IS THE DAY FOR EXCHANGING CHRISTMAS GIFTS. THIS ROSCON DE REYES – THE KINGS' RING – IS SPECIALLY BAKED FOR THE OCCASION. TRADITIONALLY IT CONTAINS A BEAN, A TINY CHINA BABY OR A SILVER COIN, AND THE LUCKY PERSON TO FIND IT IS DECLARED KING OF THE PARTY.

SERVES TWELVE

INGREDIENTS

   450g/1lb/4 cups unbleached strong
     white bread flour
   2.5ml/½ tsp salt
   25g/1oz fresh yeast
   140ml/scant ¼ pint/scant ⅔ cup
     mixed lukewarm milk and water
   75g/3oz/6 tbsp butter
   75g/3oz/6 tbsp caster
     (superfine) sugar
   10ml/2 tsp finely grated lemon rind
   10ml/2 tsp finely grated orange rind
   2 eggs
   15ml/1 tbsp brandy
   15ml/1 tbsp orange flower water
   silver coin or dried bean (optional)
   1 egg white, lightly beaten,
     for glazing
For the decoration
   a mixture of glacé (candied)
     fruit slices
   flaked (sliced) almonds

1 Lightly grease a large baking sheet. Sift together the flour and salt into a large bowl. Make a well in the centre.

2 In a bowl, mix the yeast with the milk and water until the yeast has dissolved. Pour into the centre of the flour and stir in enough of the flour from around the sides of the bowl to make a thick batter.

3 Sprinkle a little of the remaining flour over the top of the batter and leave to turn spongy, in a warm place, for about 15 minutes or until frothy.

4 Using an electric whisk or a wooden spoon, beat together the butter and sugar in a bowl until soft and creamy.

5 Add the citrus rinds, eggs, brandy and orange flower water to the flour mixture and mix to a sticky dough.

6 Beat the mixture until it forms a fairly smooth dough. Gradually beat in the butter mixture and beat for a few minutes until the dough is smooth and elastic. Cover with lightly oiled clear film (plastic wrap) and leave to rise, in a warm place, for about 1½ hours, or until doubled in size.

7 Punch the dough down and turn out on to a lightly floured surface. Gently knead for 2 or 3 minutes, incorporating the lucky coin or bean, if using.

8 Using a rolling pin, roll out the dough into a long strip measuring about 65 × 13cm/26 × 5in.

9 Roll up the dough from one long side like a Swiss roll (jelly roll) to make a long sausage shape. Place seam side down on the prepared baking sheet and seal the ends together. Cover with lightly oiled clear film and leave to rise, in a warm place, for 1–1½ hours, or until doubled in size.

10 Preheat the oven to 180°C/350°F/ Gas 4. Brush the dough ring with lightly beaten egg white and decorate with glacé fruit slices, pushing them slightly into the dough. Sprinkle with flaked almonds and bake for 30–35 minutes, or until risen and golden. Turn out on to a wire rack to cool.

INDEX